Cycling Through the Gospels

Gospel Commentaries for Sunday Bulletins

by

Jerome J. Sabatowich

Resource Publications, Inc.
San Jose, California

Editorial director: Kenneth Guentert
Managing editor: Kathi Drolet
Copy editor: Anne M. McLaughlin
Cover design: Huey Lee
Back cover photograph: Amy Sherman

Reprint Department
Resource Publications, Inc.
160 E. Virginia Street, #290
San Jose, CA 95112-5876

Library of Congress Cataloging in Publication Data
Sabatowich, Jerome, 1957-
   Cycling through the Gospels : Gospel commentaries
for Sunday bulletins
      p.   cm.
  ISBN 0-89390-207-1   : $19.95
  1. Bible. N.T. Gospels—Liturgical lessons, English.
I. Title.
BS2565.S23   1992
226'.06—dc20   91-41566
                                      CIP

5 4 3 2 1 | 96 95 94 93 92

With love to my mom and dad.

Contents

Introduction

A complete stranger walks into your church on a Sunday morning, picks up a copy of the parish's Sunday bulletin, and then leaves. Based on that parish bulletin, what picture of your faith community will this person develop?

Take a close look at your parish bulletin before you answer that question. How much space do you devote to financial news (e.g., reports on the weekly collection, announcements about bingo games or festivals, appeals for support of a diocesan collection, etc.), and how much to announcements about social events (e.g., the senior citizen trip to a shrine or a parish society's Christmas party)? Now compare that to the amount of space you give to articles of a purely religious nature (i.e., clarifications of doctrine and explanations of the day's Scripture readings). Of these three types of articles—financial, social, and religious—which one appears most frequently?

Will the stranger conclude that Jesus Christ and the Word of God are the center of your community's life? Or will this person go away thinking your parish exists to raise money or to plan social events? What kind of community image does your parish bulletin present?

Parish bulletins can be effective catechetical tools, but the sad reality is that most of them lack any kind of spiritual enrichment, focusing instead on financial matters and social affairs. The problem is that there aren't many quality resources a parish can consistently rely on to promote spiritual growth, especially in the area of Scripture study. Therefore, I wrote this book in hopes of at least partially filling that void.

These commentaries on the Sunday Gospel are short enough to fit in 1½ columns of the average weekly parish bulletin. You may consider changing the heading by replacing the words "of Ordinary Time" with "of the year." However, you should never omit the chapter and verses of the passage because those who read the commentary may want to refresh their memory by first rereading the Gospel, a habit you should encourage.

I would like to thank some special people for helping me with this project. First, there's my good friend, Colleen Gilin, who proofread the manuscript for spelling and grammatical errors and then suggested how I could make the commentaries more readable, advice that I found immensely helpful. Thanks, Neen!

Special thanks also goes to Fr. John Castelot, who spent much time reading the manuscript and pointing out areas needing work. I was very fortunate to have someone with Fr. Castelot's knowledge and background help me with this endeavor.

Finally, I'd like to express my gratitude to my pastor, Fr. Ed Scheuerman. Fr. Ed not only served as scriptural consultant when I was having difficulty explaining a verse or passage, but also gave me the opportunity to test drive my work in the weekly parish bulletin. This book would not have been possible without Fr. Ed's help and encouragement.

Cycle A

1st Sunday of Advent

Matthew 24:37-44

Christians usually call Jesus "the Son of God" but that was not Jesus' favorite way to describe himself. Jesus actually preferred the title "Son of Man," which occurs 82 times in the Gospels. To this day, Scripture scholars cannot agree about what this title means.

The book of Daniel and another Jewish writing called the Similitudes of Enoch contain the term "Son of Man." In both places, it refers to a messiah-like figure God will send at the end of the world to bring salvation and judgment to all people. Some scholars believe this term applies to an individual while others think it stands for Israel. Jesus may have used this title to identify himself as the messiah.

Some of the Jewish people expected the messiah to be a political and military figure who would lead them in battle against their enemies. They believed he would be a human being who, because he was gifted with God's own spirit, would be victorious in battle and would conquer the world. Through him, God would establish a new order in the world, in which there would be no more wars, famines, or evil of any kind. This new order is what some Jews called "the reign of God" or "the kingdom of God."

2

Although Jesus did not fight any human enemies, he did score a victory over the most important and most powerful enemy, the devil, and he promised to return one day to finish the job. When that happens, God will be in complete control of the world, and because the reign of God will be here in its entirety, there won't be any more wars or evil of any kind.

In today's Gospel, when Jesus tells us to prepare for the coming of the Son of Man he is really telling us to prepare for his own return. We do not know when this will happen so we must always be ready.

Two sentences in today's Gospel particularly interest some Christian groups. Jesus says that two men will be in the field and two women will be at the grindstone. One man and one woman will be taken and the other two will be left. Because of this passage, some Christians believe that at Jesus' second coming he will snatch up bodily those who are faithful to him and will take them to heaven so they will be spared the suffering that will take place at the end of the world. This is what some Christians call "the rapture."

For Reflection

If the world ended today, would you be ready to meet Jesus, the messiah? How will you and your family use this Advent season to prepare for Jesus' return?

2nd Sunday of Advent

Matthew 3:1-12

In ancient times when a king decided to travel through the land he ruled, he always sent his servants to prepare the way for him. These servants had two functions. First, they announced that the king was about to pass by so the people could line the streets for a glimpse of their ruler. The servants also prepared the way for the king's chariot, making sure the road was clear of all obstacles so the chariot would not have to stop unnecessarily.

Some of the Jews believed the messiah was going to be a king and, like other kings, he was going to send his servant before him to prepare his way. According to a Jewish belief based on Malachi 3:23-24, this servant was supposed to be the prophet Elijah.

In the first chapter of the second book of Kings, Elijah wears a hairy garment with a leather belt around his waist. Today's Gospel reading begins by describing John the Baptist as also being dressed this way. By drawing attention to the similar clothing worn by these two men and by quoting a verse about Elijah from the book of Isaiah, Matthew suggests that John was fulfilling the role of Elijah. John was announcing the coming of the messiah and was preparing his way just just as Elijah was supposed to.

John's message was that the Jews should prepare for the messiah by reforming their lives. The Greek word for reform is *metanoia* and it refers to a complete change in a person's life. John was telling those who came out to hear him preach that admitting their sinfulness and saying they're sorry is not enough. Their metanoia must go beyond words and must extend to how they act.

In today's Gospel, John singles out the Pharisees and the Sadducees for particularly harsh criticism because they took too much pride in being part of God's chosen people. Some of them believed that being a descendant of Abraham, the father of the Jews, guaranteed them a place of honor in God's kingdom. John warned that this was not necessarily true and that they could find themselves excluded from the kingdom unless their actions reflected their beliefs. They, too, needed to reform.

For Reflection

Is your belief in Jesus evident in how you live your life? Identify one area in which you need to reform. Work on that area during the Advent season.

3rd Sunday of Advent

Matthew 11:2-11

Some modern Christians wonder why some Jewish people in first-century Palestine did not recognize Jesus as the long-awaited messiah. The answer is that Jesus was not the type of messiah they were expecting.

Many of the Jewish people were looking for a political/military messiah who would form an army, lead them in battle against their enemies, and conquer the world. Through the messiah, God would establish his kingdom on earth, transforming the world into a new Garden of Eden where there wouldn't be any sickness or suffering. Scripture calls this period of time when God rules the world "the reign of God" or "the kingdom of God."

In today's Gospel reading, John the Baptist sends his messenger to ask if Jesus is the one who is to come or if they should expect someone else. Since the Jews sometimes referred to the messiah as "the one who is to come," John is asking if that's who Jesus is.

John, being Jewish, also anticipated a messiah who would form an army and free the Jews from foreign rule; however, Jesus did not fit this stereotype because he chose to preach about forgiveness and love of one's enemies instead of taking up arms. Thus, John was probably a little confused and must have wondered when Jesus would start acting like the messiah for whom everyone was waiting.

At first, it appears Jesus does not answer John's question because instead of coming right out and plainly saying yes or no, he points to his ability to make the blind see, the deaf hear, and the lame walk. Jesus began to restore the world to what it was like in the Garden of Eden when there wasn't any pain and suffering. Because all this is supposed to happen only after the messiah comes into the world, Jesus is saying that's who he must be. So, even though Jesus didn't perfectly fit the messianic stereotype, his answer to John's question was a definitive "yes."

For Reflection

Pretend that, like John the Baptist, you have an opportunity to ask Jesus one question about himself. What would that one question be?

4th Sunday of Advent

Matthew 1:18-24

Marriage customs in Palestine in Jesus' time were much different from what we are accustomed to today. Back then, there were two parts of a Jewish marriage ceremony—the engagement and the consummation.

The engagement, which usually lasted at least a year, was a time for the bride to make her dress and prepare for the wedding. During this period, the bride and the groom could not see each other so they communicated through messages delivered by the best man.

The engagement began with the signing of a formal marriage agreement or with the groom giving gifts to the bride's family. After this took place, the bride and the groom were legally husband and wife even though they did not yet live together.

The consummation occurred when the groom took his wife into his home to live with him. The consummation completed the marriage contract.

The story in today's Gospel tells us Joseph found out about Mary being pregnant while they were engaged but before they consummated the union. The engagement year had not ended and they were not yet living together. Since Joseph could not visit his wife during this period, she obviously wasn't pregnant with his child.

With Joseph and Mary legally becoming husband and wife at their engagement, divorce was the only way Joseph could end the relationship. Another alternative was for him to publicly accuse Mary of adultery, which, according to Jewish law, would have led to her being stoned to death. The whole mess is finally cleared up by an angel who tells Joseph Mary conceived the child by the power of the Holy Spirit. Therefore, the child has divine origin. The angel gives the child the name Jesus, a name that means "Yahweh saves" or simply "salvation." How appropriate that name is!

For Reflection

Put yourself in Mary's place: pregnant, suspected of adultery, and about to be divorced. How do you feel? How could this happen to you? What will the neighbors think? After reflecting on this, take some time today to pray for young, pregnant, unwed mothers and for those who are going through the pain of divorce.

Christmas

Luke 2:1-14

The Gospel according to Luke tells us the shepherds were guarding their flocks at night when the angels appeared to them to announce the birth of the messiah. This little detail tells us Jesus could not have been born in December, a month during which the Palestinian nights are too cold for sheep and shepherds to be out in the fields. Most likely, Jesus was born in the early spring because that was the birthing season for the sheep, a time when the shepherds would be in the fields with their sheep throughout the night just in case one of the sheep experienced a difficult delivery.

Why, then, do we celebrate Jesus' birthday on December 25? Strangely, the answer to this question lies in a pagan feast.

Some pagan peoples viewed the world as a battleground for a struggle between the powers of darkness (the evil gods) and the powers of light (the good gods). These pagans became alarmed in early December because they noticed the days getting shorter, a situation they interpreted to mean the evil gods were overcoming the good gods. Therefore, these people held a feast at which they partied and made lots of noise in an attempt to rouse the good gods from their sleep and encourage them to fight back. They celebrated this feast on December 25.

As the days began getting longer, the pagans concluded their strategy apparently worked. For them, more daylight was an indication the good gods, the powers of light, were defeating the powers of darkness. Of course, today we know longer days had nothing to do with their feast but with the winter solstice which occurs on December 22.

Some of the early Christians were once pagans who celebrated this feast with their neighbors. After they converted, they believed in one God instead of many gods who were fighting, but they were reluctant to give up the partying that they once did on this occasion. What were they to do? They solved this dilemma by giving the pagan feast a Christian meaning. This was easy to do since Jesus is the light who came into the world to overcome the darkness of sin. By adapting the feast to Christianity, the followers of Jesus were able to celebrate with their pagan neighbors without giving up their faith in the one true God.

For Reflection

The exact day Jesus was born is really not important. In fact, Jesus' birth was not even celebrated in the early days of the Church (Easter was and still is the most important Christian feast). What does matter, however, is that God became man and lived among us. Take time today to thank God for the gift of the Son.

Feast of the Holy Family

Matthew 2:13-15, 19-23

Herod the Great ruled Judea (a region in Palestine inhabited by the Jews) from about 36-4 A.D. Because the Romans who controlled Palestine sometimes sold kingdoms to the highest bidder, some historians believe Herod obtained his position of power only after making some very well placed bribes.

Buying one's way to the top often led to sleepless nights because there was always the chance someone would come along with a bigger bribe. That thought must have crossed Herod's mind because he was paranoid that someone was out to take his place as king. We know that he arrested and put to death anyone whom he suspected (including some of his own sons).

Herod must have gotten pretty nervous when the astrologers visited his palace asking where they could find the newborn king of the Jews. Because he was afraid the child they were looking for would one day take the throne away from him, Herod made plans to locate this new king and kill him. When the astrologers failed to return to him with the information he requested, Herod protected his power by killing all the boys who were two years old or younger.

Matthew also tells us that Joseph, Mary, and Jesus did much traveling because of Herod. There's a good reason why Matthew includes this detail.

In the book of Exodus, we hear about how God rescued the Jews from enslavement in Egypt and brought them back to the Promised Land (the land of Israel). Matthew goes out of his way to tell us Jesus made a similar trip from Egypt to the Promised Land as a symbolic way of saying that God is once again rescuing the people. Through Jesus, God is about to save not only the Jews, but all those who believe in him.

For Reflection

Jesus came to save all people, including Herod. Like Herod, is there anything in your life you are unwilling to ever give up? Why is this so important to you? Is it possible it is getting in the way of your salvation?

Solemnity of Mary

Luke 2:16-21

We sometimes call New Year's day the octave of Christmas. Octave means "eight"; we use it to describe this feast because it occurs eight days after Jesus' birth. Some people also call this the Feast of the Circumcision of the Lord because that is what today's Gospel is about.

Some ancient peoples practiced circumcision for hygienic reasons and others superstitiously believed circumcision warded off evil spirits. Although the Jews at first may have practiced circumcision for these same reasons, they later gave it a spiritual meaning.

Throughout the Old Testament, the Jews were conscious of the unique relationship they had with God as his chosen people. In the book of Genesis, God commands circumcision as a sign of this special covenant relationship, a sign that cannot be erased.

In obedience to God's command, the Jews circumcised their male children eight days after birth. Although we do not know if there is any religious significance to waiting eight days (as opposed to seven or some other number), we do know it is the safest time to perform circumcision because by then the body produces vitamin K (needed for the blood to coagulate) and because ten percent more prothrombin (a chemical needed for clotting) than normal is present in the body on that day. These two chemicals minimize the risk of uncontrollable bleeding resulting from the circumcision.

According to Jewish custom, the mother gave the male child his name on the day of his circumcision, a name that often described the child or an event surrounding his birth. Therefore, Mary named her son Jesus, which popularly means "God saves" or simply "salvation."

For Reflection

Today's Gospel says Mary treasured and reflected on all that was happening to her. This means she probably prayed about all the events in her life because she wanted God to be part of them. Undoubtedly, Jesus got his habit of praying from his mother. Ask Mary today to help you learn to pray like she did.

Epiphany

Matthew 2:1-12

"Epiphany means "manifestation" or "appearance." In Greek mythology, this word describes a time when a god appeared among human beings. Thus, it is appropriate that we use the term for Jesus' appearance in our world.

Matthew's Gospel is the only one containing the popular story about the wise men who follow a star to Bethlehem in search of a newborn king. Finding the house where Jesus and his parents are staying, they pay homage and give the child gifts of gold, frankincense, and myrrh. The rich symbolism in this story deserves our close attention.

The Star: Ancient people believed a new star appeared in the sky each time a child was born. Consequently, when they spotted an extra bright star they concluded someone important had been born, someone who would outshine everyone else. This was certainly true of Jesus.

Gold, Frankincense, and Myrrh: A loyal subject who had an audience with the king did not approach him empty handed but brought gifts to show appreciation for receiving such a great honor. Failing to do so would have been a breach of etiquette. Because a gift should reflect the importance of the person who receives it, only the best and most expensive gifts (like gold, frankincense, and myrrh) were good enough for a king. Gold, the most precious of metals, was especially valuable because it was so rare. Frankincense and myrrh, on the other hand, were perfumes only the rich could afford because merchants had to import them from distant lands.

Bethlehem: Many Jewish people thought the messiah would come from Bethlehem, the city King David came from, because the messiah was to be one of David's descendants. Like David, the messiah would be a military/political leader who would bring peace and prosperity.

The Wise Men: The words "magi" and "magician" ("one who has secret knowledge") both come from the Greek word *magoi,* a word that originally referred to the educated priestly class in Persia but later described any knowledgeable individual. Because *magoi* had nothing to do with royalty, we shouldn't call Jesus' visitors kings, but wise men. Being from the East (areas like Arabia or Mesopotamia), these men were not Jewish. Matthew carefully chose all these symbolic details to tell us Jesus was not just an important individual but was also the messiah-king whom many of the Jews were eagerly awaiting. Including the Gentile visitors may have been Matthew's way of saying the messiah would be for all people, not just the Jews.

For Reflection

The three wise men gave the best gifts they could possibly give to the child Jesus. If Jesus were born today, what gift would you bring?

Baptism of the Lord

Matthew 3:13-17

Some of the Jewish people in first-century Palestine were expecting God to send them a messiah who would raise an army and lead them in battle against their enemies. God's Spirit would work through the messiah to establish God's kingdom on earth, a kingdom filled with peace and justice.

In today's Gospel, Matthew says that God's Spirit descended like a dove and hovered over Jesus as he came out of the Jordan River after John baptized him. In this way, Matthew identifies Jesus as the long-awaited messiah through whom the Spirit of God would work in a special way. Therefore, with Jesus' baptism, God begins the process of establishing his kingdom on earth, a process that continues even today.

Matthew's description of the heavens opening and the Spirit descending on Jesus suggests that he is thinking of the prayer we find in Isaiah 63:7-19, a prayer composed during a low point in Jewish history—the Temple in Jerusalem was in ruins and the Jewish people were living in exile. Utterly defeated, the people turned to God, begging him to intervene in their world. The prayer ends with a plea for God to open the heavens and once again visit his people. Matthew purposely uses similar terminology, saying the heavens opened and God's Spirit descended upon Jesus, because he thinks God answered this prayer at Jesus' baptism. God was once again visiting his people.

Scripture scholars suggest that the image of the Holy Spirit as a dove may come from the second verse in the first chapter of Genesis, where we read that a mighty wind swept over the waters of the earth at the beginning of creation. The Hebrew word for "wind" can also mean "spirit of God." Thus, we can understand this verse to mean the spirit of God hovered over the earth before God began forming the world into an inhabitable planet. By using this imagery in today's Gospel, the evangelist implies that the same creative Spirit will be active in Jesus, re-creating the world into the kingdom of God through him.

For Reflection

The Spirit of God continues establishing God's kingdom of peace and justice in the world today. What are you doing to help? How can the Spirit of God work through you to promote peace in the world and in your home? How can you be the Spirit's instrument of justice for those who are poor and oppressed?

1st Sunday of Lent

Matthew 4:1-11

Fasting can sometimes be a prayer for God's help when making a difficult decision. It indicates the individual wants God's help so much that the person is even willing to suffer for it. Fasting in Jesus' day meant not eating anything from sunrise until sundown. Because one could take food after sundown, a person would not starve during a long fast like the one Jesus endured in today's Gospel.

We can assume Jesus' fast was a form of prayer for guidance from the Father. Up until that time, Jesus had spent all of his life as an obscure carpenter in a small town but was contemplating making a radical change by giving up the family business and becoming a wandering preacher. "What will my friends think and how will I support my mother? Will anyone even listen to me?" All these thoughts must have been on Jesus' mind so he brought his concerns in prayer and fasting to his heavenly Father.

Jesus' fast lasted forty days, a biblical number symbolic of transition or change (e.g., forty days and forty nights of rain in Noah's day, forty years of wandering in the desert before the Jews entered the Promised Land, etc.). After praying and fasting, the will of the Father was clear to him and Jesus knew he had to give up the quiet and secure life of a small town carpenter and take the risk of becoming a traveling preacher.

Docetism, a heresy in the early Church, said Jesus only pretended to be human, his life being an act or charade. The Church has always rejected this way of thinking and has always taught that Jesus is both God and man. This means Jesus experienced all the fears, all the anxieties, and even all the temptations other human beings experience. Today's Gospel reading tells us that even Jesus had to pray for guidance.

For Reflection

Is there anything you would be willing to fast for? Would it be for something you would not directly benefit from (i.e., world peace, healing for a sick friend, a relative's marriage, or the recovery of a neighbor who is on drugs)?

2nd Sunday of Lent

Matthew 17:1-9

Peter, James, and John climb the mountain with Jesus and something very strange happens. After Jesus changes in appearance, Moses and Elijah suddenly are present, speaking with him while a cloud overshadows them and a voice comes out of the cloud. In a matter of seconds, the vision ends.

For the Jewish people, Moses was always symbolic of the laws God gave them on Mt. Sinai, and Elijah usually represented the prophets. Together, Moses and Elijah in today's Gospel stand for "The Law and the Prophets," another name for the Jewish Scriptures.

The purpose of the Scriptures was to help prepare for the coming of the messiah, a political/military leader through whom God would establish his reign or kingdom. With God ruling the world, there would be no more pain or suffering or death.

The symbolism in the rest of the reading also deals with the reign or kingdom of God. Many Jews believed the saints in the kingdom will wear bright white clothing and will be in God's presence. In today's Gospel reading, not only does Jesus' clothing turn dazzling white but the rest of his being is transformed or transfigured as well. As Jesus converses with Moses and Elijah a cloud overshadows them, a symbol of God's presence because God led the Jews with a column of clouds when they were leaving Egypt.

Finally, Peter offers to put up three booths or tents. Because the Jews lived in tents in the desert on their way to the Promised Land, tents are symbolic of God's saving power and the Jews believed everyone in the kingdom of God will live in one.

Why all this symbolism about the reign of God? As we already said, many Jewish people (including the apostles) were expecting a political/military messiah who would establish the kingdom or reign of God on earth. Because Jesus obviously wasn't a political/ military leader, he used the event in today's Gospel to tell the apostles he is indeed the messiah even though he does not fit the stereotype. With Jesus' death in the near future, the apostles needed this assurance.

For Reflection

Even after experiencing the Transfiguration, the apostles still had difficulty believing and understanding what Jesus said. We, too, can sometimes expect to have difficulty believing or understanding what Jesus wants of us. Pray this week for an increase in faith and wisdom.

3rd Sunday of Lent

John 4:5-42

In today's Gospel reading, a Samaritan woman is surprised when Jesus asks her to give him a drink of water from the well. The reason for her surprise needs to be explained.

After King Solomon died, the land of the Jews divided into two separate kingdoms, Israel in the north and Judah in the south, with each kingdom having its own king, its own army, and its own capital. The capital in the northern kingdom was Samaria and the capital of the southern kingdom was Jerusalem, the city where the Jewish Temple was located. Citizens of both kingdoms visited the Temple because it was the only place where the Jews could offer sacrifices to God.

In 721 B.C., the Assyrians attacked and conquered the Jews of the northern kingdom and took all able-bodied Jewish men, women, and children into exile. Assyrians immigrated to the northern kingdom and some of them converted to Judaism after marrying Jewish women. Because these Assyrian/Jewish couples lived in Samaria, we call their children Samaritans.

Since the Samaritans were only half Jewish and were descendants of the Assyrians, the Jews in the southern kingdom despised them and even called them dogs.

Because of their mutual dislike, Jews and Samaritans normally did not talk to each other and some rabbis even went so far as to teach that Jews who passed through Samaritan territory should shake the dust from their feet before entering Jewish lands so Jewish soil would not be contaminated with Samaritan dust.

Since the Jewish religious leaders did not allow them to offer sacrifices in the Temple in Jerusalem, the Samaritans built their own temple on Mount Gerizim and claimed it was the only place sacrifices could be legitimately offered to God. Gerizim is the mountain the woman refers to in today's reading.

Finally, because first-century Palestinian Judaism was a male-dominated religion, some Jewish men thanked God every morning they were not females, and the rabbis occasionally debated if women had souls. The social customs of the time even frowned on a Jewish man speaking to a woman in public. When you consider all of this, it's easy to understand why the Samaritan woman was surprised Jesus talked to her.

For Reflection

Who are the people in our society others don't want to associate with? Considering today's Gospel, what do you think Jesus' attitude would have been toward these people? How do you think Jesus would want you to treat them?

4th Sunday of Lent

John 9:1-41

In first-century Palestine, physicians treated a variety of illnesses with saliva because they believed it had curative powers. In today's Gospel, Jesus approaches a man who was born blind, spits on the ground, makes a paste of dirt and saliva, and smears this paste on the man's eyes. After washing off this mixture in the pool of Siloam, the man is able to see.

Some overly legalistic Pharisees objected to what Jesus did because he did it on the Sabbath. Since they considered making paste with saliva and dirt to be work, they interpreted Jesus' actions as a clear violation of the command to keep the Sabbath holy.

The Pharisees interrogated the man born blind about what had happened, but when the man defended Jesus, they became indignant and accused him of being a sinner from the moment of his birth. Because people in biblical times did not know about viruses and germs, they believed sin was the cause of all pain and suffering. The Pharisees, therefore, concluded the man was born blind because God was punishing him for something either he or his parents did. He was a sinner, they reasoned, because he had experienced the effects of sin from the day he was born.

This story is one of seven miracles reported in the Gospel according to John. Most of these "signs" (that's what John calls them) lead into one of the seven discourses or sermons of Jesus we find in this Gospel. Although physical in nature, each miracle also has a spiritual meaning which becomes clear in the discourse that follows it.

Jesus gave sight to the blind man and this individual then preached to those who were spiritually blind (those who did not accept Jesus as the messiah). Thus, a physical cure set the stage for a teaching about the need for spiritual healing.

The reading ends with Jesus saying he came to divide the world and that some people will be blind because of him while others will regain their sight. In the original Greek language of the Gospels, Jesus clearly is not talking about the purpose of his mission but rather about its effect. There will be divisions because some people will believe in Jesus and others won't. Some of those considered spiritually blind will see Jesus as their messiah while the respected spiritual leaders will not accept him. Historically, that's exactly what happened.

For Reflection

Are you more like the blind man who needed Jesus or are you like the Pharisees who believed they were spiritually superior to others? Pray that you may see where you need spiritual healing.

5th Sunday of Lent

John 11:1-45

Throughout history, human beings have struggled with the problem of pain and suffering but have not come up with many suitable explanations. Thus, we often encourage a sick friend to accept an illness because "It is God's will," almost as if we are saying God not only wants us to suffer but also takes some kind of pleasure in seeing us in pain. Today's Gospel reading gives us reasons to question this way of thinking.

The author of the Gospel according to John provides us with a glimpse of the human side of Jesus when Lazarus, one of Jesus' close friends, dies. John tells us Jesus was troubled and wept openly upon hearing about Lazarus' death. Since this is hardly the reaction we would expect from a deity who enjoys seeing people suffer, we can conclude from this story that Jesus is a God who does not like to see his friends in pain. So, let's stop blaming him for all the evil in the world and let's stop telling people who are suffering to accept their pain because "it is God's will." It is not God's will that we suffer and die.

Where, then, does suffering and pain come from? Scripture tells us that pain, the drudgery of work, and death are consequences of sin and did not become part of life until man and woman disobeyed God (see Genesis 3). Since the devil introduced sin into the world, it is the devil, not God, who is responsible for all the pain and suffering we experience.

Finally, in today's reading, Jesus says he is both the resurrection and the life. This is just one of the seven famous "I am... " statements we find in John's Gospel. The other six are: "I am the vine and you are the branches" (15:5); "I am the bread of life" (6:35); "I am the good shepherd" (10:11, 14); "I am the way, the truth, and the life" (14:6); "I am the sheep gate" (10:7); and "I am the light of the world" (9:5).

For Reflection

Look up today's reading in a Bible. What follows this reading in the chapters immediately after this story? Why do we think the author of the Gospel put this story where he did? Hint: It's the same reason the Church uses this reading so late in the Lenten season.

Palm Sunday

Matthew 21:1-11

To understand the rich meaning of the story of Jesus entering the city of Jerusalem while riding on the back of a donkey, we first need to refresh our memories about what some Jewish authorities taught about the messiah.

The messiah was supposed to be a political/military hero who would lead the Jews in battle and defeat their enemies. Through him, God would establish his kingdom of peace and justice. Because the messiah was also supposed to be a descendant of King David, the great warrior king of the Old Testament who ruled in God's name, the Jews sometimes called him "the Son of David" or "the one who comes in the Lord's name." In today's Gospel reading, these are the same titles the people of Jerusalem use for Jesus.

When Jesus entered Jerusalem, his followers also cried out "Hosanna," a Greek word that means "save us, we pray." "Hosanna" is part of Psalm 118, a psalm associated with the messiah that the Jews recited during the Feast of Tabernacles.

Because he had royal blood in him, the Jews believed the messiah deserved the red carpet treatment. The people demonstrated this belief when they spread

30

their cloaks and branches on the ground in front of the donkey Jesus was riding. By their words and their actions, the people of Jerusalem proclaimed their belief that Jesus was the messiah for whom they had been waiting.

Jesus accepted the title of messiah, but he had his own idea of what the messiah would be. A political/military leader usually traveled on a horse, an animal used in battle because of its speed and power, but Jesus chose to ride into the city on a donkey, a beast of burden and sign of humility. In this way, Jesus indicated he was not going to be the expected triumphant military messiah but a humble servant of God who would conquer sin and death by dying on the cross.

For Reflection

Despite being in a position of power and authority, Jesus was still humble and obedient to the Father. Each day this week pray for a different person who has power and authority in the Church, in the government, or at your place of employment. Pray that these people, like Jesus, may accept their position and responsibility in humility and obedience to God's will. Reserve one day this week to pray for yourself.

Easter Sunday

John 20:1-9

All four Gospels begin their Resurrection stories not with an account of Jesus' actual rising from the dead but with the discovery of the empty tomb. Although the stories differ in detail, they all agree on the most important point—the same Jesus whom the Roman crucified is now alive!

In the Gospel according to Matthew, Mary of Magdala and another woman (also named Mary) go to inspect the tomb early on Sunday morning. There is an earthquake, then an angel dressed in dazzling white announces that Jesus is alive. After the women inform the apostles of what they experienced, Peter runs to the tomb and finds it empty. In Luke's Gospel, the resurrected Jesus first appears not to the women but to two disciples on their way to Emmaus.

In today's reading we find Mary Magdalene visiting the tomb by herself. Seeing the stone has been rolled away, Mary fears that someone stole Jesus' body, so she runs to tell the apostles. Both Peter and the beloved disciple visit the tomb and find it empty. After the apostles leave, two angels speak to Mary, and Jesus appears to her.

Mark's version has Mary of Magdala and two other women finding the tomb empty. A young man (an angel) dressed in white explains to them that Jesus has been raised from the dead and instructs them to tell Peter and the other apostles about what has happened. Unfortunately we do not have the original ending of this Gospel, so we do not know anything about what Mark says concerning Jesus' post-Resurrection appearances. The ending we do have dates back to the first century, but it is just a summary of the details we find in the other three Gospels.

Mary's role in all four Gospel stories is unusual because she appears as the hero in an event that took place in a male dominated society. It is interesting not only that the resurrected Jesus chose to appear first to a woman instead of to Peter or another apostle, but also that he chose a woman instead of a man from his inner circle to be the first to tell the others. Jesus must have had a great deal of confidence in Mary, and proving that this confidence was not misplaced, she did not disappoint him.

For Reflection

Throughout Scripture, God chooses the most unlikely individuals for his purposes. If the Resurrection took place today instead of 2,000 years ago, what type of person would be the first to experience the resurrected Jesus?

2nd Sunday of Easter

John 20:19-31

In the story of creation, the book of Genesis tells us that God formed man out of the clay of the ground and then gave the man life by blowing breath (another translation is "his spirit") into the man's nostrils. Since breath is a sign of life, this action means God was sharing his divine life with the man.

Some biblical scholars suggest John the evangelist has the story of creation in the back of his mind when he tells us Jesus breathed his Spirit on the apostles. Just as God's breath gave life to the man and the woman in the Garden of Eden, in today's Gospel the risen Jesus is giving new and eternal life to all who believe in him. Just as God shared life with the people he created, Jesus shared his resurrected life with the apostles.

Jesus tells the apostles they can forgive or refuse to forgive sins in his name. Although Christians continue to debate the meaning of this passage, its interpretation may hinge on a proper understanding of the nature of the Jewish law.

The Jewish law contains some very well defined directions about what punishments are appropriate for what crimes. If the law was very rigidly enforced, pardon for certain offenses was not possible even if there were circumstances that changed the nature of the crime. Punishment had to be meted out to the guilty party even if it was the death penalty.

Some biblical scholars suggest that, in the passage in today's Gospel, Jesus gives the early Christian community authority to forgive even sins that some Jews traditionally considered unforgivable. This, therefore, would have been a source of hope and comfort for the early Christians.

For Reflection

Are there people in your life whom you refuse to forgive? Are there people who refuse to forgive you? Pray this week for the gift of forgiveness and reconciliation.

3rd Sunday of Easter

Luke 24:13-35

Two of Jesus' disciples are walking down a road when a stranger approaches them and engages them in a conversation. Later, the disciples manage to persuade the stranger to join them at dinner. During the meal the stranger takes bread, blesses it, and gives it to them. Suddenly they realize the stranger is Jesus.

Throughout the history of Christianity, the breaking of the bread has been the most important sign of belief in Jesus. Despite great personal risk (being a Christian in the first century was illegal and was an offense punishable with death), the early Christians gathered at someone's house before sunrise on the first day of the week to share a meal that included fruits, nuts, cheeses, bread, and wine. In the course of this meal, they read from Scripture and recalled some of the things Jesus said and did but the most important action occurred when they took the bread, blessed it, and shared it with each other just as Jesus did with his apostles on the night before he died.

The breaking of the bread soon became a sign of the unity and fellowship of those who followed Jesus. Just as many grains of wheat are used to make flour and many grapes are needed to make wine, many different individuals come together to form the Christian community. Thus, sharing of the one loaf and drinking from the same cup became a visible expression of Christian unity.

Historically, Christians haven't always been as united as they should be. Disagreements over doctrine or discipline have led to splinter groups and factions that compete for converts and donations. In many ways, the unity expressed in the breaking of the bread is not a present day reality, but it is something we must continuously strive for.

For Reflection

Does unity mean all Christians must think and act the same? Is it possible for different denominations to be united in their faith in Jesus and still disagree with each other? Pray this week that Christians will have the patience, understanding, and mutual respect needed to make unity a reality.

4th Sunday of Easter

John 10:1-10

Jesus was a successful preacher because he always talked about topics familiar to people in his audience. Knowing that the most common occupations in his time were fishing, farming, and herding, Jesus told parables about casting nets into the sea, sowing seeds, and taking care of sheep or goats. When Jesus spoke about these subjects, he was sure many of the people listening would relate to what he said.

Today's Gospel reading contains a parable of interest to herders, a parable in which Jesus compares himself to a shepherd who has a very close relationship to his flock. The shepherd leads his sheep to green pastures and cool water and he protects them from wild beasts that may attack them. The sheep depend so much on the shepherd that when one of them is lost, it lies motionless and frightened on the ground until the shepherd finds it. Because a shepherd gives names to each of his sheep, he knows exactly which one is missing and begins calling out its name.

Sometimes, several shepherds brought their flocks to the same pasture and let them graze together so they could take turns watching the combined flocks. When it was time to return home, each shepherd called his sheep and they came running to him because they recognized his voice. They would not respond to the voice of a shepherd they did not know.

We are like sheep and Jesus is our shepherd. Just as the shepherd has a very close relationship with each of his sheep, Jesus wants to have a very close relationship with each of us. Just as the shepherd protects the sheep and provides for their needs, Jesus protects us and provides for all our needs. Without Jesus we could not survive.

For Reflection

The word "pastor" means "shepherd." Pray today that your pastor may be a good leader and provider of the flock entrusted to him. Pray that God will give him the courage and dedication needed to continue to be a good shepherd.

5th Sunday of Easter

John 14:1-12

Theologians sometimes describe the Church as a "pilgrim people" because Christians are like pilgrims on a journey in search of their heavenly home. Because it's easy for people to get lost when traveling to a place they've never been before, they have to look for signs and landmarks that tell them they are going in the right direction or they need someone who has already been there to point the way so they won't make a wrong turn. A person's spiritual journey is no different.

In today's Gospel story, Jesus says he is the way, the truth, and the life and that no one can come to the Father unless they come through him. This means Jesus is our guide, pointing the way to our heavenly home and calling our attention to the various spiritual signs and landmarks that tell us we are going in the right direction. Without Jesus, we can easily get lost because we do not know where we are going.

One of the lessons in today's Gospel reading also influenced formation of the Nicene Creed, a summary of beliefs of the Christian faith. In the days of the early church, there was a heresy called Arianism that claimed Jesus is not God in the same way the Father is God and that Jesus is supposedly inferior to the Father. The Nicene Creed is the Church's response to that heresy.

In this creed, we find the phrase that says Jesus is "God from God, Light from Light, true God from true God; begotten, not made, one in being with the Father." These words mean Jesus is God in the same way the Father is God. Jesus, our light, comes from the Father who is light and Jesus, the true God, comes from the Father who is true God. In other words, Jesus and the Father are one. That's exactly what Jesus means when he tells Philip in today's Gospel that whoever has seen him has also seen the Father.

For Reflection

Jesus shows us the way to the Father through his words found in Sacred Scripture. The Bible is like our map to the Father. How often do you consult this map to make sure you are going in the right direction? Why not develop the habit of putting aside ten or fifteen minutes each day to read and reflect on God's Word?

6th Sunday of Easter

John 14:15-21

In today's Gospel, Jesus calls the Holy Spirit the Paraclete, a Greek word meaning "an advocate or helper." Judges and lawyers often use this word when describing someone who helps or advises the defense in court. Jesus calls the Holy Spirit a Paraclete because the Spirit comes to our defense in our time of need.

Because being a Christian was illegal when the Gospel according to John was written, Roman authorities put on trial many followers of Jesus and condemned them to die a very painful death. While some were fed to the lions and others were crucified or skinned alive, these early Christians needed assurances that God was not abandoning them. Therefore, John says that even though they will be on trial, they will not be alone because the Holy Spirit will be at their side strengthening and inspiring them, helping them understand what is going on, and advising them about what to say. The Spirit will be with them no matter what they have to go through.

Although we are not persecuted for our faith in Jesus, the Spirit also plays an important role in our lives. We seek the advice of a lawyer not only when someone accuses us of a crime but also when we need to know the correct way to proceed on a given matter.

The lawyer points us in the right direction and gives us support and encouragement. Since it's sometimes difficult for a Christian to live in a world that does not acknowledge Jesus as God, we need the Holy Spirit to point us in the right direction and to give us advice and support so we can always choose to love God even when that's not popular.

The reading ends with Jesus telling us those who love him will obey his commands. This isn't always easy because elsewhere in the Gospels Jesus says we should love our enemies, do good to those who persecute us, turn the other cheek when someone strikes us, and give without counting the cost. Living by these standards today can be a very difficult task that we can accomplish only with the help of the Holy Spirit.

For Reflection

Pray today for those who have difficulty living out their faith in the risen Jesus, especially those who do not enjoy freedom of religion and those experiencing pressures from friends or family.

7th Sunday of Easter

John 17:1-11

The Gospel according to John contains several stories and long sermons that do not appear in the other three Gospels. Scripture scholars believe these speeches are actually John's meditations on the meaning of Jesus' life and ministry. Today's Gospel is part of one of these meditations.

The scene in today's Gospel is the Last Supper and while Jesus is at the table with his disciples (John never calls them apostles) he begins praying aloud to his heavenly Father. John uses this prayer to shed light on who Jesus is and what he has accomplished.

According to this prayer, Jesus, who existed with the Father even before the world began and who has authority over all creation, came into the world to give glory to the Father and eternal life to those who believe in him. Now that he has fulfilled this mission, Jesus prepares to entrust his message to his followers so he can return to his heavenly Father. This, in a nutshell, is John's summary of Jesus' life.

Scripture scholars have difficulty determining when John wrote his Gospel. Some of them believe it first appeared in its final form between 90-100 A.D. but others think 130 A.D. would be a more accurate date.

What they do agree on is that John was the last Gospel account written and that John wrote his Gospel after the early Christians had plenty of time to reflect on the meaning of Jesus' words and deeds.

The authorship of the Gospel is also the subject of much scholarly debate. According to tradition, the authority behind the Fourth Gospel is a man named John. Some people believe this John was John the Apostle but others remind us there were other prominent leaders of the early Church with this same name and that it would have been unlikely for any of the apostles to have lived until 90-100 A.D., the earliest date by which the Gospel is believed to have been written.

Who the author really is will remain a mystery at least for the foreseeable future because nowhere in the Gospel itself is he actually named.

For Reflection

In today's reading and throughout the Gospels, we find Jesus praying to his Father. If anybody had no need of prayer, it would have been Jesus. How important is prayer in your life? Spend a little extra time in prayer this week.

Pentecost

John 20:19-23

"Pentecost" is a Greek word that means "fifty days." It originally referred to a religious feast observed fifty days after Passover, on which the Jews thanked God for the wheat harvest. Today, Christians celebrate Pentecost fifty days after Easter to commemorate the day God sent the Holy Spirit to the early Church.

In today's Gospel, "Peace" is the first word the resurrected Jesus says to the apostles, a word the Jews used in everyday speech as both a greeting and a farewell. Jesus then shows them his hands and his side to prove that it really is him. He truly is alive!

During this post-resurrection appearance, Jesus tells his disciples he is sending them out on a mission just as his Father sent him on one. He then breathes on them and tells them he is giving them the Holy Spirit so they can go out and bring forgiveness to all people.

The word "apostle" comes from a Greek word that means "one who is sent." In today's reading, Jesus sends the apostles to tell the world about the forgiveness of sins made possible through his death and resurrection.

Breathing on the apostles like Jesus did may seem a bit crude but this action had much religious meaning.

In the book of Genesis, we read that God gave life to the first man by breathing into his nostrils (2:7) and in the book of Ezekiel (37:1-14) the prophet describes a dream he had in which a valley of dry bones comes to life with the breath of God. Because Scripture closely associates God's breath with new life, we should understand Jesus' actions in today's Gospel as him giving new life to his Church by breathing the Holy Spirit into it.

Finally, today's reading is the closest the four Gospels come to describing the arrival of the Holy Spirit on Pentecost. We are accustomed to hearing about the strong wind and the tongues of fire appearing while the apostles and friends of Jesus gathered in prayer, a story we find not in the Gospels but in the Acts of the Apostles. Matthew, Mark, and Luke all end their Gospels with Jesus promising he will soon send the Holy Spirit but only John, in today's reading, gives us an account of the Spirit actually arriving. However, since John's story is so simple and uneventful, we often overlook it.

For Reflection

How is the Spirit of God working through you when you are with your family or while you are working? Pray this week that you will become more aware of how the Spirit is working in your life.

2nd Sunday in Ordinary Time

John 1:29-34

In today's Gospel reading, John the Baptist refers to Jesus as the "Lamb of God," a title rich in meaning.

Today, when two people enter an agreement, they usually draw up a contract and sign it to make it official. In ancient times, however, this couldn't happen because most people were not able to read and write. Neither party could read the document or sign it. How then did the ancient people seal their agreements?

The answer to this question is that they made their agreements official by going through a little ceremony. They slaughtered animals, split them in two, and then walked between the two halves as a dramatic way of saying that if they weren't faithful to the terms of the agreement, may the same thing happen to them that happened to the animals. Periodically, they renewed the agreement with a similar ceremony.

Although these ceremonies differed somewhat with time and place, the one feature they all had in common was they always involved the shedding of the blood of an animal. Because ancient people believed blood was the source of life, the blood of the animal gave life to the agreement. Without the shedding of blood, the agreement was meaningless.

The early Christians believed they had an agreement with God, an agreement that, like a marriage, produced a very close and loving relationship. We call such an agreement a covenant.

The early Christians called Jesus "the Lamb of God" because his blood sealed the covenant between them and the Father. Jesus was the "animal" (the lamb) whose blood gave life to the very close and loving relationship between God and the Christian people. The crucifixion was the ceremony that made this covenant official and it is Jesus' blood that renews the covenant each time we celebrate the Eucharist. Jesus is the lamb who is slain to make possible our close and loving relationship to the Father.

For Reflection

Just as it takes much effort to make a marriage work, our covenant relationship with God also requires effort. What will you do to make your relationship with God grow stronger?

3rd Sunday in Ordinary Time

Matthew 4:12-23

In today's Gospel reading, Jesus begins preaching by telling his followers to reform their lives because the kingdom of heaven is near. This is the focus of Jesus' message.

The term "kingdom of heaven" (or "reign of God") referred to a time when, through the messiah, God's Spirit would establish a new order or kingdom in which there would be no pain, suffering, or injustice. When Jesus proclaimed the kingdom of heaven was at hand, he meant the Spirit of God was beginning the process of transforming the world. The day the Jews were eagerly awaiting was finally near.

At a time when the world didn't have telephones and televisions, Jesus needed help in getting his message across. Help came in the form of four poor fishermen who were casting their nets into the sea. Sometimes we find it difficult to understand why these men would leave everything they had to follow a wandering preacher from Nazareth but there was a good reason.

In Jesus' day, there were two different kinds of rabbis. The first kind taught Jewish boys how to read and write Scripture in the synagogue schools. The second type, called a master rabbi, taught other men how to be rabbis. A master rabbi's students probably moved in with him so they could have intense training. The master rabbi provided them with shelter and food and, in return, the students worked for him in order to earn their keep. Jesus was a master rabbi.

The Jews considered it a great privilege to study to be a rabbi. So great was the honor that anyone who had such an opportunity would not hesitate to accept it. He would commit himself on the spot because he knew his family and relatives would pitch in to assume his responsibilities so he could devote full time to his studies. That was probably what happened to Peter, Andrew, James, and John. Jesus offered them the chance to become rabbis and their families and friends would have considered them fools if they had not taken advantage of this once-in-a-lifetime opportunity.

For Reflection

A rabbi is a teacher. Pray today for all of the religion teachers who taught you about God. Ask the Father to bless them for their efforts and sacrifices. If possible, call one of them or write a letter expressing your appreciation.

4th Sunday in Ordinary Time

Matthew 5:1-12

The oral traditions were 613 man-made Jewish laws that explained the laws God gave to Moses on Mt. Sinai. These laws were supposed to be like a fence around the divine laws, protecting them from accidentally being violated. The oral traditions pertained to all parts of life and included everything from what foods could be eaten to what was an acceptable sacrifice to God.

Some of the Jews believed the oral traditions were a blueprint to holiness. Following these laws guaranteed you were holy and not following them (even if you did not know what they were) meant you were a sinner. This sort of reasoning put holiness out of the reach of the ordinary Jews. Most of them worked long hours to feed their families and didn't have time to study the laws. Because they didn't know the laws, they couldn't follow them. Because they couldn't follow the laws, they couldn't be holy. Therefore, their sufferings and sorrows were the just punishments for their sinfulness.

The rich were the only ones who had the time to learn all 613 laws. They believed their comfortable lifestyle was proof God was pleased with them. They thought God not only rewarded them for their holiness but also would give them the places of honor in his kingdom.

Jesus turns things around in today's Gospel. All the ones he says are blessed or holy are the ones people normally considered sinners. The poor who are sorrowing, or lowly, or persecuted are the ones who will be rewarded, not the rich and the powerful. What's even more astonishing is that each reward Jesus mentions has something to do with the kingdom of God.

The Jews sometimes pictured the kingdom as a new Promised Land where God would "fill the hungry with good things" and where "the sorrowing would find comfort." Those who inherit this kingdom would "see God" and would be known as "sons of God." Thus, we should understand Jesus as saying in today's Gospel that God will give the positions of honor in the kingdom to the poor and the powerless, not to the rich.

Finally, Jesus tells us that simply following laws is not enough to please God. The beatitude about the single-hearted pertains to those who serve God because they want to and not because they want a reward. In Jesus' day, some people observed the laws because they wanted others to see how holy they were. They were looking for applause and were not single hearted.

For Reflection

Are you single hearted? Why do you obey the commandments? Are you looking for a reward (e.g., heaven, a good reputation, etc.)? Would you act differently if there wasn't a life after death?

5th Sunday in Ordinary Time

Matthew 5:13-16

Jesus was a successful teacher because he always grabbed the attention of his audience by talking about something that was a big part of their lives. Many of Jesus' parables were stories about fishing, farming, and herding because those were the three main occupations in his day. Jesus knew people were bound to listen a little more attentively when he began talking about something they knew very well.

In today's Gospel, Jesus talks about salt and light because he is probably trying to get the attention of the women in his audience. The salt Jesus talks about was much like rock salt. Jewish women wrapped salt in a clean cloth and dangled it in a boiling pot of soup. When the soup was ready, they took the salt that did not dissolve and saved it for the next time they needed it. After the cook did this on several occasions, the salt lost its flavor and was only good for throwing on the wet cobblestone walks after a rainstorm. This made the cobblestones less slick.

Salt was also a preservative. Freshly slaughtered meat sold in the open air markets did not last long in the Palestinian heat unless it was salted. Like refrigeration today, salt prevented food from spoiling.

In ancient Palestine, the ordinary family lived in a one-room house illuminated in the evening by a single oil lamp on a stand. Making sure there was enough oil for the lamp was the woman's responsibility. This was very important because without this light, family members would not have been able to see what they were doing and would have had to retire to bed much earlier than planned.

As the salt of the earth, Jesus' followers not only make the world better (just as salt makes food taste better) but they also preserve what is good and holy (just as salt was a preservative). As the light of the world, they help others see God. Just as both salt and light were important in the days when there were no refrigerators and electricity, Christians are important to the world today.

For Reflection

If Jesus were to appear today, what images would he use in his parables to get people's attention? How are you salt and light to your family, your neighbors, and your friends? Is your parish salt and light to the community? If your parish were dissolved today, would anyone miss it?

6th Sunday in Ordinary Time

Matthew 5:17-37

The Pharisees, one of the main religious groups in Jesus' day, were known for their strict observance of biblical laws. In order to insure they wouldn't accidentally break one of the laws God gave to Moses on Mt. Sinai, the Pharisees made up the oral traditions, a collection of laws that went beyond the God-given laws by explaining what they meant. For instance, the Bible contains the command to keep holy the Sabbath but doesn't spell out what this means. The oral traditions filled in the gap and said we should understand this as strictly forbidding such things as lighting a candle on the Sabbath or walking more than a certain distance. The other biblical laws were dealt with in a similar manner.

The Pharisees believed their oral traditions were just as important as the laws Moses got from God and to break one of them was as serious as breaking the law itself. Therefore, whoever broke either a divine law or one of the oral traditions was a sinner.

Jesus objected to the oral traditions because they became more important than human beings. For instance, observing the oral traditions was sometimes an excuse for not assisting someone in need on the Sabbath, even if failing to help meant the person suffered needlessly. Jesus acknowledged there were circumstances when the oral traditions not only could be but should be ignored. Because of this, his enemies often accused him of ignoring the Jewish law. Jesus answers this accusation in today's Gospel.

The law said not to commit murder but Jesus said we should not even get angry. The law said not to commit adultery but Jesus commanded his followers not even to look lustfully at another person. The law permitted divorce but Jesus didn't. The law said not to take a false oath but Jesus said not to swear at all. Thus, today's Gospel makes it clear that the charge that Jesus ignored the Jewish laws was false. Instead, Jesus consistently went beyond the demands of the law.

For Reflection

It isn't easy to love someone who always makes you angry but that is what Jesus demands of us in today's Gospel. Pray this week for someone with whom you do not get along. Think of some specific ways you can love that person.

7th Sunday in Ordinary Time

Matthew 5:38-48

Today's Gospel is a continuation of last week's reading. Again, Jesus answers the charge that he is teaching his followers to disregard the Jewish law. In response, Jesus shows he demands even more than what the law demands.

The quotation about taking an eye for an eye and a tooth for a tooth is from Exodus 21:24 and is one of the most misunderstood passages in Scripture. Although people usually quote it when trying to justify revenge, its original purpose was to prevent unjust punishments by placing limits on the penalty imposed on a convicted criminal. Therefore, the authorities could not put the guilty party to death for knocking out someone's tooth. The worst thing they could do to him was knock out his tooth also. Thus, this passage was never intended to be a recommendation about what a punishment *should* be but only a limitation on what it *could* be. The punishment could never exceed the crime.

Although the law permits revenge, Jesus does not advocate it. In explaining that his followers should not offer resistance to injury, Jesus says they should give not only their shirt to someone who wants it but their coat as well. The coat was an outer garment a person slept in at night. Although Palestinian days were usually warm, the temperature often dropped dramatically after the sun went down. The coat was all the poor man had to keep him from freezing at night and it was so important that, according to Jewish law, if a man gave his coat as collateral for a loan, the lender was supposed to return it to him before nightfall so he wouldn't freeze to death.

In his preaching, Jesus sometimes used exaggeration, an accepted Near Eastern teaching technique, to stress an important point. Jesus' comments in today's Gospel about giving up one's coat and in last week's Gospel about gouging out one's eyes if they are a source of temptation are examples of exaggeration. Thus, in today's reading Jesus is not saying that his followers should deliberately expose themselves to physical harm but that they are to forgo any revenge they might be entitled to and should even be willing to put up with injustice for the sake of the kingdom of God.

For Reflection

It is difficult for us to respond to hate with love but that is what Jesus is asking of us in today's Gospel. If there is someone in your life you hate, go out of your way this week to do something nice for that person.

8th Sunday in Ordinary Time

Matthew 6:24-34

A king demands total and undivided loyalty from his subjects who pledge their allegiance to him and promise to serve him all their lives. In turn, the king protects and takes care of them, showing special concern for the poor, the homeless, and the needy.

In today's Gospel reading, Jesus tells us to seek the Father's kingship over us and assures us the Father will take care of us if we acknowledge him as our Lord and King, giving him our undivided loyalty and trust. As proof, Jesus points to the loving care the Father bestows on the birds of the air and the flowers of the field. If God takes such great care of his less significant creations, we can trust he will give us all we really need.

The Church has taken today's Gospel reading and those of the last few Sundays from the Sermon on the Mount (chapters 5-7 of Matthew). In the Gospel according to Luke, Jesus delivers this same sermon not on a mountain but on a flat stretch of land, leading biblical scholars to wonder if the mountain in Matthew has any special significance.

Most of the early Christians were originally Jewish and one of the biggest events in the history of the Jewish people was Moses receiving the Ten

Commandments and the rest of the Jewish laws on top of Mt. Sinai. The Jews treasured these laws as the way to holiness, a blueprint explaining how a person could have a close relationship with God.

Matthew's symbolism was clear to the early Jewish Christians. Just as Moses ascended to the top of Mt. Sinai to get the laws from God, Jesus ascends to the top of a mountain and gives the people a new law, a new way to holiness, making Jesus a new Moses. Just as Moses was the mediator between God and the Jewish people, Jesus is the mediator between God and all people. Just as Moses showed the Jews the way to the earthly Promised Land, Jesus shows us the way to the heavenly Promised Land. Moses was the most important figure in Jewish history and Jesus is the most important figure in the history of the world. The early Jewish Christians recognized all these similarities and more.

For Reflection

Human beings spend time on anything important to them. Make a list of everything you did yesterday and how much time each activity took. How much time did you spend praying, reading Scripture, and learning more about your faith? Does the amount of time you spent getting to know God better indicate your relationship with him is important to you?

9th Sunday in Ordinary Time

Matthew 7:21-27

The Sermon on the Mount, from where the Church takes today's and the past few weeks' Gospel readings, ends with Jesus warning his disciples that they cannot be content with merely saying they are his followers. Rather, their faith in him must be evident in both what they say and in what they do. This admonition applies not only to ordinary Christians, but also to those individuals whom God has chosen for a special task.

God has given all of us certain gifts (charisms) we can use for the building of his kingdom. However, some people possess extraordinary abilities that set them apart from others. These individuals may have the gift of prophesy, the power to work miracles, or some other charism. Jesus tells us in today's Gospel that these God-given gifts do not guarantee holiness. These people still must struggle to live the Gospel message in their lives. They still must work at being the kind, forgiving, and loving individuals God calls them to be.

We can assume Jesus' words apply to all sorts of people, including those who have authority and power within the Church. Modern Christians have a tendency to put church leaders on a pedestal as if they are holier than the ordinary person by virtue of their position. We forget that they, too, are subject to such temptations as lust, pride, and arrogance. Rather, we expect them to be perfect and immune to all human weaknesses. All we have to do is study our history books to see how foolish this way of thinking really is.

What is interesting about today's Gospel is that Jesus said those who prophesy *in his name*, heal *in his name*, and work miracles *in his name* are not guaranteed a place in the kingdom of God. To speak or act in someone else's name means you get power and authority from that person. It is as if that person is speaking and acting through you and is bound by what you say or do. Therefore, allowing someone to speak or act in your name involves putting a great deal of trust in that person and with this trust comes the responsibility to represent you as best as possible. This means that anyone who speaks or acts in Jesus' name has the responsibility to represent him by becoming more like him. This person must strive to be as loving, forgiving, and patient as is Jesus himself. Because this isn't an easy task, our spiritual leaders need our prayers, our support, and our patience as they, like us, struggle to overcome their human weaknesses.

For Reflection

Pray for the spiritual leaders of your congregation. Pray they will continue to become more Christ-like so they can effectively speak and act in Jesus' name.

10th Sunday in Ordinary Time

Matthew 9:9-13

If tax collectors are not very popular today, we can be assured they weren't very popular among the Jews in Jesus' day either. However, the reasons why they weren't well liked back then are a little different from our modern day reasons.

Because the Jewish people believed God was their king, they also believed all their tax money should be used for the upkeep of God's palace, the Jewish Temple. In Jesus' day, however, the Romans controlled Palestine and the Roman emperor declared himself to be the only king of the land. This infuriated the Jews because they thought the emperor was trying to take God's place.

The Jews were even more angry when the emperor demanded they pay taxes to him. They believed the emperor was stealing from God because he was taking the money that should have been used for the Temple. The Jews especially despised the tax collectors for helping the emperor do this.

Tax collectors also had a reputation for being dishonest and greedy. When they didn't reach their quota of taxes collected, the difference came out of their own pay. Thus, tax collectors often tried to collect more than they were supposed to. Whatever amount they got over their quota usually ended up in their own pockets.

Finally, the only thing worse than a tax collector was a tax collector who was a Jew. The Jews considered such a person a great sinner and a traitor because he was one of God's chosen people who was now stealing from God.

In today's Gospel, Jesus invites a Jew who was a tax collector to follow him and become one of his disciples. Imagine how stunned the Pharisees must have been! Instead of asking a holy and respected Pharisee to be one of his followers, Jesus chooses a despised sinner. Let us be thankful Jesus continues to want to associate with us sinners!

For Reflection

Why do you think Jesus chose a tax collector to be his disciple and not someone who appeared to be holy, like a Pharisee? If you were Jesus, would you have chosen to associate with a tax collector?

11th Sunday in Ordinary Time

Matthew 9:36-10:8

As the owner of a large company, you have just hired an ad agency to promote your product. You'll probably expect the agency to recruit someone famous to be your company's spokesperson but if that's not possible, you'll at least want your company represented by people who are attractive, well respected, reasonably intelligent, and able to get the message across. These expectations would be normal. Considering these criteria, we might wonder why Jesus chose the people he did to be his spokesmen.

Today's Gospel reading contains a list of the twelve apostles, some of whom were fishermen from Galilee. Making a living casting nets into the sea was a strike against them because most fishermen in Jesus' day could neither read nor write. They were most likely poor, ill-mannered, and a little rough around the edges.

Being from Galilee didn't help either because Galileans were the ancient world's version of the Beverly Hillbillies. They were low class, they talked funny, and they weren't very well respected.

As for the rest of the apostles, many of them were shady characters. Matthew was a tax collector and tax collectors were not very popular in Jesus' day because most people suspected them of collecting more than they were supposed to and then pocketing the extra money.

Simon was a Zealot, a member of a political party that hated the Romans. Zealots had a reputation for assassinating their political enemies with a well-placed knife in the back. Because they were sometimes called the *sicarii*, a name that means "knife," and because Iscariot is a form of the word *sicarii*, some scripture scholars believe Judas may have also been a Zealot.

Finally, the apostles weren't very brave or dependable. One of them betrayed him. Another denied knowing him and they all ran away when Jesus was arrested. Thomas didn't even want to believe Jesus had been raised from the dead. When we consider all this, it's amazing Jesus' message actually did get preached.

For Reflection

Throughout Scripture, we have examples of God choosing to work through the weak and the helpless rather than those who are strong. Who are the weak and the helpless in your life that God is using to speak to you?

12th Sunday in Ordinary Time

Matthew 10:26-33

In today's Gospel reading, Jesus tells us to be afraid of anyone who can destroy both our body and soul in Gehenna. Gehenna is the Jewish name for the underworld and it is sometimes also called Hades or She'ol.

The Jewish people in Jesus' day believed the earth was flat and they pictured Gehenna as the area beneath the earth where all people went after they died. There were three layers to Gehenna and the layer a person ended up in depended on one's deeds while on earth.

The top layer was a place where the deceased waited twelve months until the consequences of their actions were clear. Those who God judged to have led a good life remained in the top layer awaiting their reward at the end of the world, but those who led wicked lives were sent to one of the two lower layers. The specific layer depended on the nature of the crimes committed.

Some rabbis believed God showed mercy on the Sabbath by quenching the fires, but other rabbis thought the flames were continuous.

Christians called Gehenna "hell," and in the Apostles' Creed we say Jesus descended into hell before rising from the dead. This means Jesus visited the top layer of Gehenna to take to their reward those whom God had already judged righteous.

For Reflection

How would you describe hell? Would you act differently if you found out there wasn't a hell? Why or why not?

13th Sunday in Ordinary Time

Matthew 10:37-42

Jesus says that he who welcomes a prophet will receive a prophet's reward. For many of us, this passage has little or no meaning because we somehow have the idea that God doesn't send prophets into the world anymore. That's simply not true. The problem is that we do not understand what a prophet is.

We associate prophets with gazing into the future, but Scripture tells us the real role of a prophet was to advise and admonish the king, especially on matters pertaining to justice. The prophet pointed out to the king that the poor were being treated unjustly or that widows and orphans were being neglected. The prophet confronted the king about discrimination and spoke for those who could not speak for themselves.

If the king did not attempt to solve the problem, the prophet would warn him of the dire consequences that would result. "If you continue to neglect the poor," the prophet would tell him, "the Lord God will neglect to bless you." Of course, all this did not make the prophet very popular with the king and it occasionally resulted in the prophet's early death.

When we understand the role of the prophet in this way, we can see that there are prophets in the world today, people in our society who speak out on behalf of the poor and the needy by calling our attention to the plight of the hungry and the homeless. These people may work hard to protect the elderly from abuse and they might cry out against the build up of nuclear arms. These are the modern day prophets Jesus encourages us to welcome.

Like the prophets of the Old Testament, today's prophets work for justice and they challenge us to do the same. We may not agree with the positions they have taken on certain issues but we owe them our respect because they are not just talking about faith in God but are trying to make God's love and concern for his children a reality.

For Reflection

Anyone who can write a letter can be a prophet. Take time this week to write to an elected official to ask what is being done about the hunger problem, nuclear armament, affordable housing for the poor, etc. Encourage this elected official to speak out for those who cannot speak for themselves.

14th Sunday in Ordinary Time

Matthew 11:25-30

Many of Jesus' parables are about fishing, farming, and herding because those were the three most common occupations in his day. The parable in today's Gospel reading is aimed at getting the attention of the farmers in Jesus' audience.

In this parable, Jesus says we should take his yoke upon our shoulders and learn from him. A yoke, a type of harness a farmer uses to attach a couple of oxen to a plow or a wagon, looks like the McDonald's golden arches over the shoulders of the two animals. With the yoke attached, the oxen share the burden of pulling the plow or the wagon.

If one of the oxen is old or sickly, the other ox has to work harder. Sometimes the farmer will team a young ox with an older, more experienced ox so the younger one will learn from the older one how to pull the yoke. Until the younger one gets the hang of it, the older ox must do most of the work.

When Jesus says we should take his yoke and learn from him, he is offering to share our burdens with us. With Jesus helping us, our burden will be light and easy to pull. Just as the two oxen work side by side, Jesus is willing to walk beside us and help us as we travel through life. We do not have to face life's problems all by ourselves.

Because our society values independence, most of us want to prove we can succeed on our own. This pride not only drives us further from each other, but it also drives us further from our God. In our obsession to do it by ourselves, we shut out all help from everyone else, even help from Jesus.

Maybe that's why Jesus praises the Father for taking what was hidden from the learned and the clever, and revealing it to the children. The learned and the clever are those who are self-sufficient and less likely to accept Jesus' help because they'd rather try to succeed on their own. Children, on the other hand, have no problem with being dependent on others. They are accustomed to looking around for assistance and are therefore more likely to turn to Jesus in their moment of need.

For Reflection

Identify one area in your life in which you pride yourself at being independent. Do you include Jesus in that part of your life? Pray this week that you, like a child, would become dependent on Jesus.

15th Sunday in Ordinary Time

Matthew 13:1-23

Methods of farming in Jesus' day were very different from the methods modern farmers use. Today's farmer plows the field before scattering the seed, but in biblical times farmers reversed the process. The first-century farmer scattered the seed on the ground first and then turned over the soil. We must keep this in mind when reading today's Gospel.

Because the seed rested on top of the ground for a while before the farmer plowed the soil, the wind sometimes blew it to an area the farmer did not intend it to be. This explains how some of the seed landed on the foot path and how some of it ended up on the rocky ground or among the thorns.

In the analogy in today's Gospel, the seed represents the word of God and the different places where the seed landed represent different kinds of people and their response to the Gospel message. The rocky soil stands for the person who hears God's word but does not allow it to take root. Letting the seed take root means letting the Gospel message make a difference in a person's life. It means living out one's commitment to Jesus by feeding the hungry, clothing the naked, and visiting the sick or lonely.

Some of the seed landed among thorns which represent worldly cares like fame, power, and money. When these become the center of a person's life, there isn't much time or energy left for prayer and spiritual matters.

Some seed landed on the footpath. This symbolizes the person who hears God's word but doesn't take time to study Scripture and, therefore, doesn't understand it. As a result, the Gospel message cannot make much of a difference in this person's life.

Finally some of the seed fell on good soil where it produced a yield of thirty-, sixty-, or a hundred-fold. The good soil represents people who are spiritually fruitful because they not only hear God's word but also understand it and live it. Since a farmer in Jesus' day would have been extremely proud of such a large harvest, we can assume Jesus is proud of us when his word takes root and grows in our lives.

For Reflection

How well rooted is God's word in your life? Does it find life in what you do and how you treat others? Do you spend time reading and studying Scripture? How often do you pray?

16th Sunday in Ordinary Time

Matthew 13:24-43

Scripture scholars agree that the evangelists did not write the Gospels until many years after the events took place. For instance, the Gospel according to Matthew was probably written around 85 A.D., almost fifty-five years after the death and resurrection of Jesus.

We know that the early Christians passed on the Gospel stories by word of mouth before actually writing them down. This surprises some people because they reason that a story is bound to get distorted if it is passed on verbally. That was not as great a danger in the early Church as it is today.

Because most people back in those days were not able to read and write, they had to rely on their memories much more than we do. Therefore, they developed memory techniques that made it easier to recall long lists and detailed stories. Some people were even able to give a two or three hour speech without using notes and without forgetting anything.

One such technique involved linking thoughts or themes. Something in one story reminded the person of the second story and something of this second story reminded the person of the third story. This might be why the three seemingly unrelated parables in today's Gospel reading appear together.

The parable about the man planting seeds reminded the early Christians about the story of how a mustard seed grows into a huge bush. This second story about growth, in turn, reminded them of the parable about how yeast makes dough grow. Thus Matthew grouped these three parables together to make it easier for the early Christians to remember them when verbally teaching others about what Jesus said and did. This means that Jesus did not teach these three parables in this order or even at the same time.

Sometimes it's not obvious why certain stories or parables appear together because the connection may be clear only in Greek, the original language of the Gospels. A certain Greek word in one parable may sound like another Greek word in the following parable and so forth. In any case, we must remember that the stories we have in the Gospels did not originally belong in the order they appear.

For Reflection

What group of people do you think each of the parables in today's Gospel was aimed at? Whose attention did Jesus hope to get?

17th Sunday in Ordinary Time

Matthew 13:44-52

Last week we talked about how the evangelists did not write the Gospel accounts until many years after the events took place. You may wonder why the early Christians did not immediately record what Jesus said and did. The answer to this question is quite simple.

The early Christians expected Jesus to return to the earth within their lifetime so he could defeat all evil, conquer the world, and then fill the world with peace and justice. This second coming of Jesus (also known as the *parousia*) would signal the beginning of the reign of God and the end of the world.

Believing that the end of the world was near, the early Christians did not consider it necessary to write down what Jesus said and did. They expected the apostles and those who knew Jesus to live until he returned, which would insure that Jesus' teachings did not get distorted.

When the world did not end as soon as expected, the followers of Jesus feared that all of the eyewitnesses would be dead before he returned and there would be no one left to guarantee the accuracy of the stories about him. Therefore, they decided to write down Jesus' works and teachings so future generations of Christians would have a reliable account.

Finally, let's take a look at the parables in today's Gospel. In the first parable, the man sells *all* he has so he can buy a field containing a buried treasure. In the second parable, the merchant sells *all* he has so he can buy a valuable pearl. The treasure and the pearl stand for the reign of God. Just as both the man and the merchant gave up everything when they found what they wanted, Jesus encourages us to be willing to give up everything for the sake of God's kingdom.

That's exactly what the early Christians did. Some of them suffered persecution and some of them even died for their faith in Jesus. Recalling these parables gave them the courage they needed to give up all they had, even their lives, for the growth of the reign of God.

For Reflection

How much we are willing to give for something depends on how valuable it is to us. How much would you be willing to sacrifice for the kingdom of God?

18th Sunday in Ordinary Time

Matthew 14:13-21

The story of Jesus feeding a large crowd with a couple of fish and a few loaves of bread is the only miracle story we find (with a few minor changes) in all four Gospels. In fact, since both Mark and Matthew tell it twice, it appears a total of six times. It's logical, then, for us to ask why this story is so important. There are two answers to this question.

First, the Jewish people often pictured the reign of God (also known as the kingdom of God) as a huge banquet of the finest food. Those invited to attend this feast will eat all they want and no one will go away hungry.

Most biblical scholars believe there is a connection between Jesus feeding so many people and the reign of God. Just as Jesus gave earthly food to those who followed him, he will one day feed us with heavenly food when he returns to establish his rule over the earth. The miracle, then, is a promise that those who believe in Jesus will have a place at the banquet in God's kingdom.

This miracle may also refer to another meal, the Eucharist, in which Jesus promises us everlasting life in the kingdom of God. If Jesus was able to give his followers the earthly food they needed to stay alive, then we can count on him to give us the heavenly food (his body and blood) in the Eucharist for our spiritual life and growth.

Understanding that this miracle refers to both the reign of God and the Eucharist solves only part of the problem. We must now turn our attention to why both Matthew's and Mark's Gospel each contain this story twice.

In one account in both of these two Gospels, we find Jesus preaching to the Jews and in the other, he is preaching to the Gentiles. This is significant because some of the rabbis taught that the reign of God will be only for the Jewish people. Matthew and Mark each repeat this miracle story with Gentile audiences to point out that God's kingdom will be for all people. No one will be excluded.

For Reflection

Sharing a meal has always been a sign of friendship. Take time today to thank God for the people with whom you share your food. Pray that one day all of you will share a meal in the heavenly banquet of the reign of God.

19th Sunday in Ordinary Time

Matthew 14:22-33

Today's Gospel reading begins with Jesus going away by himself to pray, a common event in the Gospels. Many times we read of Jesus retreating to the desert or climbing up the side of a mountain so he could be alone while praying to his heavenly Father. Why, we may ask, was prayer so important to Jesus?

Most married couples who have been together for a long time say that communication is one of the secrets to a successful relationship because without it, their relationship could never have grown and would never have survived. Communication is so important that the relationship begins to die as soon as communication stops.

Sometimes communication is verbal (e.g., saying "I love you"), but at other times husband and wife communicate by the way they look at each other. Sometimes communication is an action (e.g., going out to dinner together) or it may be just being with the other person. What we must remember is that two people who love each other don't ask if they must communicate. Rather, they want to communicate because that is what makes their relationship grow.

What does all this have to do with Jesus praying to his Father? If we define prayer as communicating with God, then just as communication is necessary for a relationship between two people to grow stronger, it is also important in one's relationship with God. The more a person prays, the stronger that person's relationship with God becomes. Just as a human relationship will die without communication, a relationship with God will also die without prayer.

In today's Gospel, Jesus retreats to a quiet place because his relationship with his Father is important to him, a relationship that would have weakened without regular prayer. In this sense, Jesus needed to pray but, because he loved his Father and because people who love each other want to communicate, he also wanted to pray so his relationship with his heavenly Father would grow stronger.

For Reflection

If communication does not have to be verbal, what are some of the non-verbal ways in which we can pray to God? What actions communicate to God that we want to make him happy?

20th Sunday in Ordinary Time

Matthew 15:21-28

The Jews had every reason to be proud that they were God's chosen people. After all, they were God's instruments and God was working through them in a special way. However, because of this pride, some Jews looked down at other people as being inferior and sometimes they even referred to Gentiles as dogs.

Some Jewish leaders thought this special relationship with God entitled them to certain honors and privileges. They believed the messiah (also known as the Son of David because he was supposed to be a descendant of King David) would come only for the Jewish people. Through him, God would lead them in battle, defeat their enemies, and establish his kingdom on earth. As a Jew, Jesus was familiar with this belief.

In today's Gospel reading, a Canaanite woman calls Jesus the Son of David. Although she is not Jewish, she acknowledges Jesus as the messiah because she wants him to heal her daughter.

At first, Jesus does not reply to the woman. Later, he explains to her that he, the messiah, is supposed to go to just those who belonged to the house of Israel (the Jews). The woman persists but Jesus does not give in. He replies that he cannot throw the food of the children (the Jews) to the dogs (the Gentiles), echoing the popular belief that the messiah is just for the Jews.

The Canaanite woman is stubborn and she reminds Jesus that even the dogs get what the children do not want. The suggestion is clear. If the Jewish leaders won't accept him as the messiah then maybe Jesus should turn to the Gentiles. Historically, that's exactly what happened.

In the Acts of the Apostles and in St. Paul's epistles, we find that the apostles first preached to the Jews but then turned to the Gentiles when fewer Jews than expected put their faith in Jesus. Like the woman in today's Gospel, many Gentiles accepted Jesus and, as a result, Christianity spread throughout the world.

For Reflection

Carefully reread today's Gospel. What reason does Jesus give for granting the woman's request? Pray this week that you will become more like the Canaanite woman.

21st Sunday in Ordinary Time

Matthew 16:13-20

In today's Gospel reading, Jesus first asks his disciples what others are saying about him and then he asks them for their own opinion. The various answers to this question tell us there must have been some debate about the meaning of Jesus' ministry.

Some people believed Jesus was John the Baptist. Although King Herod killed John, many people who saw the signs and miracles Jesus performed wondered if he might really be John resurrected. Other people thought Jesus was Jeremiah or Elijah.

Jeremiah was a great Old Testament prophet who took the Ark of the Covenant (the box in the Temple containing the Ten Commandments) and hid it in a cave on Mt. Nebo just before the Babylonians conquered Jerusalem in 586 B.C. (2 Maccabees 2:4-8). Since no one ever found the Ark of the Covenant, some Jews believed Jeremiah would return to the earth just before the messiah's arrival to reveal where he hid it. Thus, Jeremiah's reappearance would indicate that the time of the messiah is near.

Elijah was the greatest of the Old Testament prophets. According to the second book of Kings, Elijah never died but went to heaven in a fiery chariot. Some

Jews believed Elijah would one day return to the world to prepare the way for the messiah. When Elijah appears, the messiah will not be far behind.

The people showed great respect for Jesus when they compared him to these three great men but they did not recognize him as the long awaited messiah. Only Simon Peter understood that Jesus was even more important than the greatest of the Old Testament figures and his belief in Jesus as the messiah earned him a place of honor in the early Church. Simon Peter's faith is the sturdy rock on which the Church is built.

For Reflection

Close your eyes and pretend Jesus is asking you who *you* think he is. What is your answer? Be honest!

22nd Sunday in Ordinary Time

Matthew 16:21-27

Today's Gospel reading begins with Jesus explaining that he is about to suffer and die. Peter responds much as any of us would in that situation and tells Jesus not even to think that would happen. Peter was probably surprised when Jesus reacted angrily. Why did Jesus object so strongly to Peter's words? What was wrong with Peter's response? These are questions we must answer before we can begin to understand today's Gospel reading.

In last week's Gospel, Peter was the first to recognize that Jesus was the messiah. Jesus praised him for this insight and said Peter was the rock on which he would build his Church. Now, suddenly, Peter goes from hero to goat. The reason for Peter's quick fall probably lies in what he meant when he called Jesus the messiah.

Being a typical Jew, Peter probably thought much like many of the other Jews of his day who were expecting a military and political messiah who would lead them in battle against their enemies and eventually conquer the world. Peter thought it was only a matter of time before Jesus began forming an army to achieve this objective.

Jesus' talk about suffering and dying did not fit in with the popular beliefs about a triumphant messiah. Therefore, Peter took Jesus aside and tried to straighten him out by saying something like, "Teacher, you've got it all wrong. You're the messiah and the messiah is a winner. What you're describing is a loser. So, stop talking about such nonsense."

It's obvious that Peter and Jesus had different ideas of what the messiah was supposed to be. Jesus was the type of messiah who would not look for success on the battlefield but rather would be triumphant in another way. Instead of defeating human enemies, Jesus was going to conquer both death and the father of death (the devil). This spiritual victory would be more important than any earthly triumph Peter or any of the other Jews could imagine.

Even though the apostles were with Jesus every day and knew him better than anyone else, they still took time to grasp what he was saying. Their privileged position was not enough to guarantee immediate understanding of who Jesus was and what he was about.

For Reflection

How do you think Peter felt after the incident in today's Gospel reading? If you were Peter, would you have continued to follow Jesus?

23rd Sunday in Ordinary Time

Matthew 18:15-20

We have never found the original manuscripts of the four Gospels, but some very old copies do exist. In our oldest copies of the Gospel according to Matthew, today's reading is a little different from what we heard proclaimed in church. In the sentence that talks about what to do if your brother commits some wrong against you, the words "against you" are not there. This indicates that someone other than the original author added these words. How and why did this happen?

Since printing presses and copying machines were not available in the first century, a scribe copied an important document by hand. He would sit down with a quill pen and a scroll of papyrus and copy the document letter by letter. Occasionally, the scribe would make a mistake and leave out a letter or phrase, but sometimes he tried to make a passage clearer by adding his own words. That's what may have happened with today's reading: a Christian scribe added the words "against you" to clarify what Jesus said.

In today's Gospel, Jesus outlines a three-point plan we should follow to lovingly correct a fellow Christian we observe doing something wrong. If, however, the guilty party still refuses to repent, Jesus tells us to treat that person like a Gentile or a tax collector.

A Gentile is anyone who is not Jewish. Many of the Jews did not associate with Gentiles, and some of the rabbis even taught that a Jew traveling through Gentile territory should shake the dirt from his sandals before stepping on Jewish soil so as not to contaminate Jewish land.

Tax collectors were even worse than Gentiles. Because the Jews considered God their king, they thought their tax money should be used for the upkeep of God's house(the Temple). Because the tax collector gave the tax money to the emperor, the Jews believed he was stealing from God. Therefore, the Jews had nothing to do with tax collectors. A Jew who touched a tax collector was ritually unclean and could not offer sacrifices in the Temple.

Treating an errant person like a Gentile or a tax collector is a last resort. The reading clearly stresses that we should give the sinner every opportunity to repent.

For Reflection

Reread today's Gospel and write down the three steps in how to lovingly correct another person. Strive to follow these steps whenever you are upset with someone. Notice that gossip is not one of the steps.

24th Sunday in Ordinary Time

Matthew 18:21-35

In the first two chapters of the book of the prophet Amos, we find God choosing not to punish various nations until they commit their fourth offense. God patiently forgives them on the first three occasions but his wrath flares up after that. Since we cannot expect a human being to be more patient and merciful than God, the rabbis of Jesus' day concluded that no one had an obligation to forgive anyone more than three times.

Peter came out of last week's Gospel looking pretty bad, but in today's reading he tries to repair his tattered image by asking Jesus how many times he should forgive his brother. Being a good Jew, Peter knew he could not be expected to forgive anyone more than three times.

Without waiting for Jesus' response, Peter asks if seven times is enough. He probably was looking for a pat on the back for being very merciful, and he undoubtedly wanted Jesus to praise him for his willingness to go beyond what was expected of him. Instead, Jesus goes one step further and tells him to be ready to forgive seventy times seven times.

Jesus did not literally mean we should forgive others 490 times (70 x 7= 490). The phrase "seventy times seven" was symbolic of a great number, meaning we should always be ready to forgive. There must be no limit to our mercy.

Notice that the rabbis reasoned that the number of times a person should forgive is dependent on the number of times they believed God forgives us. Since God supposedly forgives three times, humans also should forgive three times. In the parable in today's Gospel, Jesus' reverses this logic by teaching that God's forgiveness depends on our willingness to forgive others. If we forgive those who have offended us, God also will forgive us. However, if we hold a grudge or seek revenge, we cannot expect God to show us mercy. We have to forgive before being forgiven.

For Reflection

Is there anyone who has hurt you whom you refuse to forgive? If so, carefully think of the words in the Our Father. Can you still say "and forgive us our trespasses as we forgive those who trespass against us" and not forgive that person?

25th Sunday in Ordinary Time

Matthew 20:1-16

Because people in biblical times built walls around their city for protection from hostile invaders, the only way anyone could get in or out was through the city gate. The area just inside the gate was a busy place because that was where the elders met to settle the disputes of the city's residents, traders sold their goods, and men gathered looking for work.

In today's Gospel, Jesus tells a parable about a vineyard owner who went to the city gate at daybreak, midmorning, noon, mid afternoon, and late afternoon to hire men to help with the harvest. The younger and stronger workers undoubtedly got jobs first. Those who were still around later in the day were the men who could not work as fast or do as much because of old age or poor health. These men were unemployed simply because no one hired them.

When it was time for the vineyard owner to pay the workers, he gave each of them a full day's wage; those hired first felt cheated because they worked longer and harder than those hired later in the day. Naturally, the laborers who worked all day thought the vineyard owner should have paid them more than the ones who did less work. We can sympathize with these men, but we should also consider the predicament of the others.

A man needed at least a full day's wage to feed himself and his family for one day. If a man did not find a job, his wife and children would have to go without food and his neighbors would ridicule him because he wasn't able to provide for his household. Therefore, the owner of the vineyard showed compassion for those he hired last by paying them more than they deserved.

The moral of the parable is clear. The owner of the vineyard is God and we are the workers. Because our God is compassionate, we can expect him to give us our daily bread. He will provide for all people, even for those who are lowly and not wanted. All we need to do is put our trust in him.

For Reflection

Take a few moments today to thank God for his generosity. Thank him especially for necessities such as a roof over your head, food on your table, or clothes on your back, because many people in the world today do not have these things.

26th Sunday in Ordinary Time

Matthew 21:28-32

In today's Gospel, Jesus says the tax collectors and prostitutes will enter God's kingdom before the chief priest and elders. As you can imagine, the chief priest and elders were probably not very happy when they heard this.

As the spiritual leader of the Jewish people, the chief priest officiated at worship services on Jewish holy days, was the main religious teacher, and had the responsibility of protecting the Jewish law. Because the chief priest represented the entire community, the Jews believed he should be holier than anyone else.

The elders were older Jewish men respected for their wisdom. They usually made up the town council, the city's main governing body. Also known as the Sanhedrin, the town council passed laws, enforced these laws, and even tried those who were accused of breaking the laws. The Jerusalem Sanhedrin is the group that arrested Jesus and determined he should die.

So, it appears Jesus was aiming his comments at the Jewish people's religious leaders, who were regarded as very holy men and were supposed to be an example to the ordinary Jew. Because of their holiness, most people believed the chief priest and elders would occupy the places of honor in God's kingdom.

The prostitutes and the tax collectors were the exact opposite. As public sinners, despised by their fellow Jews, they were to occupy the lowliest spots if they ever made it to the kingdom of heaven. They certainly weren't in the same league as the chief priest and the elders.

We are now ready to understand the meaning of Jesus' comments. The chief priest and the elders said they were holy, but like the first son in the parable, they did not back up their words with action. They refused to repent when John the Baptist urged them to do so.

The tax collectors and the prostitutes who accepted John's teaching and reformed their lives are like the second son who ended up doing his father's will. Because of this, Jesus says they (not the chief priest and the elders) will have a prominent place in the kingdom of heaven, implying that the tax collectors and prostitutes are holier than the chief priest and elders. As you can imagine, Jesus angered the Jewish leaders so much they began to look for a way to put him to death.

For Reflection

The saying "actions speak louder than words" can sum up today's Gospel reading. You say you believe in Jesus. What are some of the actions that back up these words? Be specific.

27th Sunday in Ordinary Time

Matthew 21:33-43

Jesus tells a parable about a man who planted a vineyard and put a hedge around it and then dug a vat and erected a tower. The owner built the hedge out of prickly plants and rocks to keep wild animals out of the vineyard. He also erected a vat for crushing the grapes and he hired a watchman to stay in the tower to guard against enemies who might steal or damage the crop.

The owner then leased the vineyard to tenant farmers, men who cared for and harvested the grapes before making the wine. Because they did not own the land, the tenant farmers agreed to give the vineyard owner a certain percentage of their crop. According to the law at that time, if a vineyard owner died without having any sons, the vineyard would become the property of the tenant farmers.

When harvest time came, the vineyard owner sent his servants to collect his share of the crop. The tenant farmers beat one of the servants, stoned another, and killed a third. The owner sent more slaves, but the same thing happened. The owner finally sent his only son, thinking that the tenant farmers would respect his flesh and blood. Alas, they killed his son too. Furious, the vineyard owner drove out all the tenant farmers and leased the land to others.

This parable is really a summary of how the leaders of the Jewish people treated Jesus. The vineyard is the kingdom (reign) of God. The owner is God himself. The original tenant farmers are the Jewish leaders. The servants are the prophets of the Old Testament. The new tenant farmers are the Gentiles (a Gentile is anyone who is not Jewish).

God sent the prophets to the Jewish people but their leaders mistreated and even killed them. God finally sent his son, Jesus, but they killed him too. Because the Jewish authorities rejected Jesus as the messiah, God then offered the reign of God to the Gentiles. The despised Gentiles became the new heirs to God's kingdom.

For Reflection

The Jewish leaders believed they were assured a special place in the kingdom of God because they were God's chosen ones. The parable points out that wasn't the case. How many times do we act or think this same way simply because we are Christian?

28th Sunday in Ordinary Time

Matthew 22:1-14

To understand the parable in today's Gospel, we have to remember that Jesus addressed it to people who had no modern conveniences like gas or electric stoves, refrigerators, and supermarkets. Preparing a huge banquet was a difficult and time consuming task because the host could not possibly plan everything so the food would be ready exactly when the guests arrived.

Because of the work involved, the host usually sent two invitations. The first informed the guests they were being invited to a banquet, but it did not include a specific time for the feast because the host could not be sure when the food would be done. This advance notice gave the guests time to wash up and change into appropriate clothing so they would be prepared for the second invitation when all the food was ready.

The Jewish rabbis often used the image of a wedding banquet to symbolize the reign of God. Some of them believed that God would invite only the Jews to this banquet and that the leaders of the Jewish people would occupy the places of honor because of their holiness.

In this parable, Jesus is the king's son for whom the banquet is given, and the invited guests are the Jews. The servants are the prophets of the Old Testament and those gathered from the byroads and the alleys are the Gentiles. The meaning of the parable should now be clear.

Through the prophets, God told the Jewish people to prepare for the coming of the reign of God, but because their leaders refused to recognize Jesus as the messiah, God extended the invitation to the Gentiles. With this parable, Jesus infuriated the Jewish chief priest and elders because the Jews despised the Gentiles and believed the Gentiles would not share in the reign of God.

In the parable, the king sends his servants to burn the city of the guests who did not come. This was probably not part of the original story but a detail Matthew added years later. In 70 A.D., the Romans destroyed Jerusalem, the center of Jewish worship. Because Matthew wrote the Gospel after this event took place, biblical scholars believe he added the detail about the burning of the city as an explanation that God allowed Jerusalem's destruction because the Jewish authorities refused to accept Jesus as the messiah.

For Reflection

Reread the parable in today's Gospel. Notice the excuses the guests gave for not going to the banquet. What is keeping you from accepting an invitation to a closer relationship with God?

29th Sunday in Ordinary Time

Matthew 22:15-21

In today's Gospel reading, some of the Pharisees (a group of very strict Jews) along with a few Herodians (Jews who supported King Herod and advocated Jewish cooperation with the Romans) ask Jesus if it is alright to pay tax to the emperor, a question they are sure will get Jesus in trouble because it puts him in a very delicate situation.

In Jesus' day, the Romans ruled Palestine and when the Roman emperor declared himself to be the only king of the land he issued his own coins as a sign of his authority. Because the Jews believed God was their king, they were outraged because they thought the emperor was trying to take God's place. Since using a coin with the emperor's image on it would have been like acknowledging his sovereignty over them, the Jews minted their own coins and used Roman coins only when they had to (e.g., when paying taxes to the Romans).

Since God was their king, many Jews also believed their tax money should go for the upkeep of God's house, the Temple in Jerusalem, but the Romans insisted the Jews pay taxes to the emperor, a practice that offended the Jews because they believed the emperor was stealing from God. To make matters even worse, the emperor then used some of this money to build pagan temples. You can see that the Jews had good reasons for not wanting to pay taxes to the Romans.

If Jesus responds to the question posed by the Pharisees and Herodians by saying the Jews should not pay taxes, he knows the Herodians will report him to the Romans and they will arrest him. However, if he says paying taxes is acceptable, he will offend many of his Jewish followers. It looks like Jesus is in a no-win situation.

Just when he seems trapped, Jesus asks the Pharisees and Herodians whose image is on the coin. Since the answer is "Caesar's," Jesus reasons that it then must belong to Caesar and should therefore be returned to him. This story suggests Jesus did not object to paying taxes to the emperor.

For Reflection

Pray this week for the leaders of our country. Pray that they will use our tax money wisely.

30th Sunday in Ordinary Time

Matthew 22:34-40

In today's Gospel, the lawyer who asks Jesus the question about the greatest commandment is from a group of religiously strict Jews known as the Pharisees. Members of this group believed in angels and life after death but we know them best for their observance of what they called the oral traditions.

Because the Jews believed the laws in sacred Scripture were a blueprint to holiness, anyone who obeyed the laws was holy. Anyone who did not obey them, even if they did not know what the laws were, was a sinner. Therefore, the Pharisees tried to avoid accidentally breaking the laws by protecting them with more laws. These man-made laws, known as the oral traditions because they were originally passed on verbally, encircled the biblical laws like a fence, preventing a person from even coming close to breaking one of them. The Pharisees believed the oral traditions were just as important as the laws in sacred Scripture.

Of the 613 oral traditions, 248 were positive ("You shall...") and 365 were negative ("You shall not..."). Depending on what they pertained to, some of these laws were light and others were heavy. The lawyer in today's Gospel asks Jesus which of the laws was the heaviest or most important. Jesus' response is a combination of two verses—one from Deuteronomy and the other from Leviticus.

The verse from Deuteronomy 6:4-5 about loving God with our whole heart, soul, and mind means we should not hold back anything when loving God. This verse is the first Scripture passage Jewish boys memorize; many Jews consider it a summary of the entire Jewish law. The pious Jew recites this passage every day when he or she wakes up.

The second verse about loving our neighbor is from Leviticus 19:18. Jesus' answer is unique because when he says we cannot love God without also loving our neighbor, he makes these two commands equally heavy. Most rabbis, on the other hand, would have argued that loving God was more important.

We find the logic behind Jesus' teaching spelled out in the first epistle according to John. In 4:20, the author tells us that if we aren't able to love a brother or sister we can see, we certainly aren't able to love the God we cannot see. Love of God and love of neighbor go hand in hand.

For Reflection

Pretend you have just died and you are standing before God's throne. God tells you he will let you into heaven but first you must tell him about one concrete action you did on a regular basis that showed you loved your neighbor. How would you respond?

31st Sunday in Ordinary Time

Matthew 23:1-12

Deuteronomy 6:4-5 tells us to love God with our whole heart, our whole soul, and our whole mind. Immediately following this passage we find the command to bind these words to our wrist and let them be as a pendant on our forehead. The Jewish people took this command literally, made little black boxes (called *tephillin* or phylacteries), and placed handwritten copies of Deuteronomy 6:4-5 and other verses in them. They then tied one of these boxes to their foreheads and another to their wrists with leather straps.

In Deuteronomy 22:12, God commands the Jews to wear fringes on the borders of their garments. These fringes and four tassels, one on each of the four corners of the outer garment, were to remind the Jews of God's commandments. In Jesus' day, some Jews wore wide phylacteries and big tassels to call attention to themselves.

In today's Gospel, Jesus criticizes some of the Pharisees for wanting the places of honor in the synagogue. Because the location of a person's seat reflected social status, the most important people usually sat in the front of the synagogue and the least important sat in the back. Therefore, everyone was sure to notice a dignitary arriving and making his way to his front just before services began.

Finally, Jesus talks about how some of the Pharisees liked to be called "Rabbi," a title that means "my master" or "my teacher." In first-century Palestine, a person's social status was also evident by how others addressed him. The more important the person, the longer and more elaborate the greeting.

Jesus bases his objection not on the meaning of the word "rabbi" but on the common opinion that a rabbi was more important and deserved more respect than one's own parents because the rabbi passes on spiritual life through his teachings while parents are only able to give physical life to their children. For this the rabbi received longer and more elaborate greetings in public places.

Because all of the practices Jesus mentions in today's Gospel were ways people could call attention to their own holiness, we should understand Jesus' comments as a warning against using religious acts to enhance our reputation.

For Reflection

Pray this week that God will grant you true humility and purity of intention so all you say and do will be said and done for his glory and honor, not yours.

32nd Sunday in Ordinary Time

Matthew 25:1-13

In first-century Palestine, Jewish wedding celebrations were very special events involving the entire town. The festivities began after dark with the bridegroom and his friends making their way to the house of the bride. As they walked through the dark streets, members of the wedding party carried torches of oily rags wrapped atop brass poles. They often needed an extra supply of oil to keep these torches lit.

The groom usually tried to catch everyone by surprise by keeping secret the day and the time he chose to claim his bride. However, someone usually went ahead of the wedding party to announce that the groom was on his way.

The bride joined the procession when the groom arrived at her house and—accompanied by much singing, dancing, and merry making—they returned to his home for both the wedding ceremony and the seven day celebration that followed. During this return procession, people came out of their homes and into the street to join the festivities and to offer their congratulations to the happy couple.

Once the wedding party arrived at the home of the groom, only the invited guests went inside. Because the door was barred shut with a heavy beam, making it difficult to open and close the door, latecomers were not allowed in. This explains why the bridesmaids in today's Gospel were not admitted to the celebration when they arrived at the groom's house. The ceremony had already begun and removing the beam not only would have been a chore but the resulting noise would have disrupted the proceeding. Thus, the foolish bridesmaids missed the long-awaited wedding ceremony because they were unprepared.

The Bible often uses a wedding as an image for the reign of God. In the parable in today's Gospel, just as no one knows the time of the bridegroom's arrival, so no one knows the day or the hour Jesus will return to the earth to establish the reign of God. It could be today, tomorrow, next year, or ten years from now. Since no one knows when Jesus will return, everyone should always be prepared and should not be caught sleeping like the bridesmaids in today's Gospel parable.

For Reflection

What does it mean to be prepared for Jesus' coming? If Jesus returned to the earth right now, would he find you ready and waiting?

33rd Sunday in Ordinary Time

Matthew 25:14-30

When you find a difficult story in the Bible, reading what comes immediately before and after helps since the evangelists often grouped parables or stories together because they had something in common. For example, a parable preceded and followed by stories about judgment probably also has something to do with being judged. The parable in today's Gospel reading is a perfect example of this.

The parable is about a man who gave three of his servants different sums of money and then went on a journey. When he returned, he summoned his servants and demanded an accounting of the funds he had entrusted to them. The master was pleased with the first two servants who doubled their money but he was furious with the third servant who had the same amount he started with. The master then took the money from this last servant and gave it to one of the others.

Taken by itself, it's difficult to determine what this parable is supposed to mean. Whom does the master symbolize? Who are the servants supposed to stand for? What is the moral of this story? These are questions we can best answer only after examining the context in which we find the parable.

Other parables and stories about the reign of God and Jesus' second coming precede and follow today's Gospel. They are about judgment and our relationship with others. It's logical to assume the parable in today's Gospel has a similar theme.

The master stands for Jesus, and we are the servants. The money represents the talents and abilities God has given us. Just as the master went away for awhile and then returned, Jesus will one day also return to the earth and will demand an accounting of the gifts God has given us. He will ask if we used our talents and abilities for good or for evil or if we wasted them by not using them at all. How we answer these questions will determine if we will share in the master's joy (be called into God's kingdom) or if we will find ourselves in the darkness outside, wailing and grinding our teeth (experience the pains of hell).

For Reflection

Make a list of all your talents and abilities. How can you use these talents and abilities to give greater glory and honor to God?

Trinity Sunday

John 3:16-18

In today's reading, Jesus explains to us the real reason he came into the world. He did not wish to condemn us or to scare us into obeying God's laws, but rather to show us he loves us and wants us to respond to that love by loving him in return. The Bible often compares this love between God and his people to the love between a husband and wife.

A husband who knows his wife doesn't like to pump gas, fills the tank before she uses the car. A wife who doesn't like science fiction movies attends a Star Trek film festival with her husband because that's his favorite show. The husband and wife do these things not because they have to but because they want to express their love for each other.

Our relationship with God is very similar. Just as the husband and wife communicate their likes and dislikes to each other, God communicates his likes and dislikes to us through Scripture and just as the couple show their love for each other by doing certain things and avoiding others, we show our love for God by doing what pleases him and avoiding what makes him angry. That sounds simple enough but, in reality, showing our love for God is often very difficult.

Sometimes we think of the Ten Commandments simply as a list of do's and don'ts and maybe only reluctantly follow them because we don't want to go to hell when we die. When this is how we view the Commandments, we are forgetting the reason God gave them to us.

Because the Commandments are God's way of telling us what pleases him and what does not please him, obeying them is like the wife watching Star Trek or the husband pumping gas. Following the Commandments, then, shows our love for God. If we understand them in this way, we will no longer ask if we have to obey them but will want to obey them because that is what loving God is all about.

For Reflection

People who love each other want to spend time together. How much time do you spend with Jesus?

Corpus Christi

John 6:51-58

As the Jews wandered through the desert after escaping from Egypt, they started grumbling because they did not have enough food to eat. God heard their complaint and provided them with bread from heaven, which they called *manna.*

God saved his people from starvation by feeding them much like a mother feeds her children with food they need to grow strong and healthy. Therefore, the Jews considered manna to be a symbol of God's saving power and a sign of his great love for his people.

In today's Gospel reading, Jesus compares his body and blood in the Eucharist to the manna his Father gave the Jews in the desert. Jesus' body and blood is special food from heaven which, like the manna, is evidence of God's saving power and his great love.

Although Jesus' body and blood and the manna are similar, they are not identical because those who ate the manna in the desert still died but those who eat Jesus' body and drink his blood will have eternal life. Therefore, Jesus' body and blood in the Eucharist is greater than the manna and is an even better expression of God's saving power and love for his people.

Jesus promised those who eat his flesh and drink his blood will rise from their graves. This promise is the foundation for the Christian belief that at the end of the world we will rise from the dead just as Jesus rose from the tomb on Easter Sunday morning. Like Jesus' resurrection, our own resurrection will be bodily and not just spiritual.

For Reflection

If we do not eat, our physical body will weaken and we will eventually die. What will happen to our spiritual selves if we do not partake of spiritual food?

Christt the King

Matthew 25:31-46

The scene in the parable in today's Gospel reading is
the judgment at the end of the world. The parable
begins with a reference to the Son of Man coming in his
glory. The term "Son of Man" refers to the messiah, the
military/political leader through whom God would
rule the world and establish his kingdom. The messiah
will come in his glory at the end of the world when he
will be victorious over all his enemies.

In the parable, Jesus says that the messiah will sit
upon his royal throne and all the nations will assemble
before him as he separates them into two groups like a
shepherd separates sheep from goats. In Palestine, the
shepherd usually allowed the sheep and the goats to
graze together but separated them whenever he took
them home or moved them to another pasture.

The king/messiah tells those he places on his right
side that he will give them a spot in God's kingdom
prepared for them since the beginning of the world.
According to the Jewish rabbis, God created his
kingdom even before the world began and those he will
judge righteous he will reward with everlasting life in
this kingdom while the wicked he will send to a place
of fire reserved for the devil and his followers.

Notice that Jesus does not say judgment will be based on how well known or popular a person is, how much money or power one has, or even where someone worships, but on how the individual responds to those who are in need. By telling us that whenever we do something for others we are really doing it for him, Jesus identifies himself with those who are suffering and is saying that to serve God we have to serve each other. We cannot separate our responsibilities to our neighbor from our responsibilities to God.

This parable should make us a little uncomfortable because it means we cannot sit back and expect to enter heaven simply because we believe in Jesus and go to church every Sunday. Jesus demands more from his followers. He demands we live out our faith in service to others. Unless our faith finds expression in visiting the lonely, comforting the grieving, feeding the hungry, and clothing the naked, we cannot expect to enter into the kingdom of heaven.

For Reflection

How balanced is your spiritual life? Do you find time to be with God *and* with those who are in need? Do you express your faith by serving those who are less fortunate?

Cycle B

1st Sunday of Advent

Mark 13:33-37

As the Advent season begins, Jesus reminds us in today's Gospel that we must always be ready because we do not know the day or the hour when he will return to the earth. In Greek, the original language of the Gospels, *parousia* is the word for the second coming of Jesus.

The early Christians believed the parousia would occur within their own lifetime. Jesus would return to conquer the world and the world as we know it would end. With Jesus in complete control, the reign of God would begin and there would be no more wars, hunger, or suffering. God would then transform the earth into a new garden of Eden, just as it was before the first sin.

This belief in Jesus' imminent return caused a problem for the early Church. Some Christians who concluded there wasn't much sense in working if the world was going to end some time soon, relied on others to support them while they spent their time praying and waiting for the parousia. This led the author of the second letter to the Thessalonians to lay down the rule that anyone who would not work should not eat (3:10).

The belief in Jesus' quick return also delayed the writing of the Gospel stories. Instead of recording what Jesus said and did, the early Christians verbally passed on stories about Jesus. They were not afraid that Jesus' teachings would get distorted because they expected the parousia to occur before the apostles and other eyewitnesses were all dead. One of them would always be around to insure the accuracy of what was being said.

Only after it was clear that the parousia was not going to occur as soon as they first thought, did the early Christians finally begin writing the Gospels. Because of this, the first Gospel (Mark) was not written until about 65-70 A.D. That's thirty-five to forty years after the death and resurrection of Jesus!

For Reflection

The early Christians went to an extreme by believing the parousia would occur at any minute but most modern Christians act as if the world cannot end in our own lifetime. Today's Gospel reading warns that this isn't necessarily true.

2nd Sunday of Advent

Mark 1:1-8

In 2 Kings, we find Elijah, one of the most important figures in the Old Testament, clothed in the traditional garb of a prophet, a garment of camel's hair with a leather belt around his waist. Because 2 Kings 9 tells us that God took Elijah up to heaven in a whirlwind, some of the Jewish people believed God was saving Elijah for a special mission and that one day God would send him back to the earth to prepare the way for the messiah.

The author of Mark's Gospel begins today's reading by quoting a passage from the prophet Isaiah that the Jews often understood as referring to Elijah's return and he also informs us that John the Baptist dressed the same way Elijah dressed. In this subtle way, the author tells us that John the Baptist fulfilled the role of Elijah. He was the one God sent to prepare the way for Jesus, the messiah.

In the first sentence of the first chapter of Mark, the author calls his work a Gospel about Jesus, who is both the Christ and the Son of God. The word "gospel" means "good news," and Mark is the only one of the four evangelists to refer to his writing in this way.

The word "Christ" means "Anointed One," a title the Jews used for the messiah. This reference to Jesus' being both the Christ and the Son of God indicates the Gospel is not an unbiased account of the life and times of Jesus of Nazareth. It is clear that Mark is a person of faith who wants to share that faith with others. This type of writing is called "salvation history," a term biblical scholars use to describe an account of how God is working in the world.

Finally, some Jewish people went to the Jordan River to be baptized by John. For many Jews, baptism was a sign of sorrow for one's sins and an indication the person would try harder not to offend God. It was not a requirement for being a member of the Jewish faith.

For Reflection

During Advent, the Scripture readings remind us to prepare for Jesus' coming. We are not awaiting the appearance of a baby in a manger but rather, an adult Jesus who has been victorious over sin and death. If Jesus came for you right now, would you be ready? What can you do this Advent season to get ready?

3rd Sunday of Advent

John 1:6-8, 19-28

In today's Gospel, priests and Levites went to ask John the Baptist who he was. Unlike our modern day priests, the Jewish priests were not chosen for the job because they were specially trained or because they were particularly holy but because they were descendants of Moses' brother Aaron. In Exodus 28:1, God commanded Moses to consecrate Aaron and Aaron's sons as priests of the Jewish people. From that day on, only Aaron's descendants were to represent the Jewish people when offering sacrifices in the Temple.

The Levites were descendants of a man named Levi, one of the twelve sons of Jacob, whose descendants make up the twelve tribes of Israel. Because God gave the Levites the special honor of assisting the priests in the Temple, some of the more menial tasks (e.g., cleaning up and filling the lamps with oil) were their responsibility.

As you probably remember from last week's reading, some of the Jewish people expected the prophet Elijah to return to the world to help prepare for the coming of the messiah, a political/military leader through whom God would rule the world and establish his kingdom. John emphatically said that he was neither the messiah nor Elijah.

124

John also denied being the Prophet. Deuteronomy 18:15 and 18:18, says that one day God will send the Jewish people another prophet like Moses. Since Moses talked directly to God (Exodus 34:27-35), many of the Jews considered him the greatest prophet who ever lived. The Prophet, like Moses, would be a very special person.

If John the Baptist wasn't the messiah or Elijah or the Prophet, then who was he? Today's Gospel describes him as a man God sent to point to the light. This light was Jesus.

The first five books of our Bible make up the Jewish Torah. The rabbis sometimes called the Torah a light because the laws found in the Torah illuminated the way to holiness. Anyone who observed all these laws was close to God and, therefore, holy. By identifying Jesus as the light, John says that it is Jesus who lights the way to holiness, not the Jewish laws. Only through Jesus can we establish a very close and loving relationship with our Father in heaven.

For Reflection

Sometimes we consider ourselves good Christians because we do what the Church tells us. Church laws are good but they cannot replace Jesus. If we want to be holy, we must have a close and loving relationship with Jesus. There's no other way.

4th Sunday of Advent

Luke 1:26-38

The word "messiah" never appears in today's Gospel; however, the author implies it throughout. The Jews expected the messiah to be a descendant of David, whom Luke refers to in today's Gospel and whom we hear about in today's first reading. David was, at one time, the king of the Jews and a great military leader.

According to 2 Samuel 7, David felt guilty that he lived in a luxurious palace while the Ark of the Covenant (the box containing the tablets of the Ten Commandments) was kept in a tent. Because the Jews believed God was present wherever the ark was, David wanted to build a house (Temple) for both the Ark and the Lord. David abandoned his plans after the Lord revealed to the prophet Nathan in a dream, that he, the Lord, would build a house for David instead. God said this would not be a physical house but a royal household of people. David's kingdom, according to God, would endure forever and his throne would always be firm. The Jewish people believed this meant one of David's descendants would always govern them.

Long after David's death, one enemy after another conquered the Jews, killing their kings and then ruling over them. Since God would not lie and was always faithful, many Jews concluded they had misunderstood the promises he made to David. They reasoned that God would one day fulfill his promises through one of David's descendants. This person would be the messiah.

That is why Luke carefully tells us that Mary was engaged to Joseph, a descendant of David, and that Mary's child would one day occupy David's throne. With these references, Luke shows us that legally (through Joseph), Jesus was a descendant of David and was also the messiah. Jesus would rule over the house of Jacob (also called Israel; his twelve sons' descendants make up the twelve tribes of Israel), a rule that will never end.

For Reflection

When Mary agreed to God's request to be the mother of the messiah, God didn't tell her of all the sufferings and disappointments she would experience. Rather, she put her total trust in God's care. Pray this week that you too will find the strength to trust the Lord completely.

Please refer to Cycle A for the following commentaries:

Feast of the Holy Family

Luke 2:22-40

Today's Gospel talks about two important Jewish religious practices—the purification of a woman after childbirth and the presentation of a male baby in the Temple. Because these two Jewish rituals play an important role in today's Gospel, we must take a closer look at each of them.

The Purification: The ancient Jewish people believed God was the source of life, using blood as a vehicle to communicate that life to human beings. Therefore, a person who came in contact with blood came in contact with God's creative power. Since this experience of God set the person apart from the ordinary world, this individual had to undergo a purification before returning to everyday life. This purification, usually a ritual bath, restored the person to "normalcy" before offering sacrifices to God or taking part in religious services.

Jewish women, therefore, underwent a ritual bath after each monthly period. After childbirth, the woman also offered a year old lamb and a pair of pigeons or turtledoves at her purification. However, if the woman was poor, she offered only the birds. This explains Mary's offering in today's Gospel.

The Presentation: When the Jews were slaves in Egypt, God appeared to Moses and told him to lead his people to freedom. When the pharaoh refused to let the Jews go, God punished the Egyptian people with ten plagues, the last being the death of the first born Egyptian male in each family. Because God spared the Jews from this catastrophe, they believed their firstborn sons belonged to God (Exodus 13:11-16) and "ransomed" these sons back with an offering of five shekels (coins). In today's Gospel, Joseph and Mary fulfill this Jewish law when they visit the Temple for Mary's purification.

Today's Gospel concludes with Joseph and Mary returning with Jesus to Nazareth in Galilee. Galilee, a region within the land of Palestine where most of Jesus' ministry took place, was a relatively small area, only about forty-five miles long from north to south.

For Reflection

Jesus, Mary, and Joseph's first recorded family outing had a religious purpose. How often does your family pray and attend church services together?

Baptism of the Lord

Mark 1:7-11

Today's Gospel reading begins with John baptizing in the Jordan River, a practice the Jewish people understood differently than Christians today. For many Jews, baptism was a symbolic gesture of repentance, demonstrating sorrow for offending God and intent on changing for the better. This ceremonial washing was rich in symbolism. John was baptizing where the Jordan River flowed into the Dead Sea, an ideal spot because at certain times of the year this part of the Jordan was both narrow and shallow. The people who came to John entered the Jordan from one shore and after John totally immersed them in the water (he did not simply pour water over their heads) they exited onto the opposite shore where they put on a fresh set of clothes. These simple actions spoke louder than any words possibly could.

Since people in first-century Palestine did not have running water, they did not bathe as frequently as we do today. To make matters worse, Palestinian days were hot and the terrain was dry and sandy. Although sponge baths were common, they simply did not compare with immersing one's entire body in water. The only way a person could get really clean was by visiting one of the public bath houses or by jumping into a nearby lake or river.

Those who came to John for baptism were giving up their sinful ways (symbolized by the dirt and the sweat on their bodies) which they washed away when John immersed them in the water. They further dramatized this clean start by entering the Jordan from one shore and exiting onto the other, indicating they were not going back to their old way of life but were leaving their sinful habits behind. Finally, they put on fresh clothing to show they were embarking on a fresh start.

This symbolism points to Jewish baptism marking a change in a person's life. Therefore, Jesus probably wanted John to baptize him even though he never sinned because the baptism marked the beginning of his new lifestyle. Jesus was about to leave behind the private life of a simple carpenter and begin his public ministry as a rabbi. From that point on, Jesus' life would never be the same again.

For Reflection

The change in your life that began at baptism continues today. What in your life do you need to leave behind so you can be more pleasing to God?

1st Sunday of Lent

Mark 1:12-15

Today's Gospel reading is short but full of rich symbolism. A look at the meaning behind the symbolism helps us better understand the message of the story.

The reading begins with the Spirit sending Jesus out into the desert, where Satan tempts him for forty days. While Jesus is in the desert with the wild beasts, angels wait on him.

In the Bible, the number forty is symbolic of transition or change. In Noah's day, the rains came down upon the earth for forty days and forty nights. After the Jews escaped from slavery in Egypt, they wandered through the desert for forty years before entering the Promised Land. Therefore, the author uses the forty days Jesus spends in the desert to alert us to a change that is about to occur in Jesus' life, a change in which he gives up the security of the carpentry business to become a traveling preacher.

Mark, the author of the Gospel, tells us this transition in Jesus' life is more than just a change of professions because it also involves a battle between Jesus and his troops (angels are symbolic of God's army) and the devil (Satan) and his army (wild beasts symbolic of evil spirits). Jesus and his forces are about to mount an attack on the devil's own territory (the desert is the dwelling place of evil spirits) in a winner-take-all main event in which the prize is control over the world.

The most vivid image of the struggle between Jesus and the devil appears in the miracles Jesus performed. Not knowing about germs and viruses, the people of Jesus' day believed demons or evil spirits caused sickness. Therefore, each time Jesus healed someone, he defeated not just the sickness but also the devil that caused it. Each miracle, then, was another victory for Jesus in his war against the devil.

According to Scripture, the struggle between Jesus and the devil is going on even today and will continue until Jesus ultimately defeats Satan and takes control of the world. When that day comes, the world will be completely in the hands of God and there won't be any more pain or suffering or death. God will then restore the earth to what it was like before man and woman sinned.

For Reflection

Jesus' resurrection proved he is more powerful than the devil. Examine your conscience and identify one sinful habit in your life. Pray this week that Jesus will help you overcome this weakness.

2nd Sunday of Lent

Mark 9:2-10

In today's Gospel, Peter, James, and John witness something very strange when they climb to the top of the mountain with Jesus. Without warning, Jesus' clothing becomes dazzling white while both Moses and Elijah appear and talk to him. A voice comes from a cloud overshadowing the group. Within seconds, the vision ends.

This vision is rich in symbolism. Moses represents the Jewish laws while Elijah represents the prophets. Together, they stand for "The Law and the Prophets," another name for the Jewish Scriptures. The purpose of the Scriptures is to prepare for the messiah through whom God will rule the world. With God in control, there will be no more pain or suffering or death. The Jews called this the reign or the kingdom of God.

The cloud overshadowing Jesus and his visitors would have reminded the apostles of the column of clouds God used to lead the Jewish people out of Egypt. Thus, the cloud is symbolic of God's presence.

The symbolism in the remainder of the reading also deals with the reign of God. The Jews pictured the saints wearing bright white clothing in God's kingdom, which is exactly how Jesus is dressed.

Finally, Peter offers to erect three tents (or booths). Because the Jews lived in tents when they were in the desert on their way to the Promised Land, tents were a symbol of God's saving power. Some Jews believed everyone will live in tents in the kingdom of God.

This symbolism about the reign of God is very important because it points to Jesus being the messiah even though he will not live up to popular expectations. Instead of being the victorious military leader some Jews were waiting for, Jesus was to die the cruel and painful death of a common criminal. By everyone's standards, Jesus was a failure.

In today's Gospel, it is clear the apostles do not grasp the meaning of what Jesus is telling them because as they come down from the mountain we find them discussing what Jesus meant when he said he would rise from the dead. They were still looking for a victorious political/military messiah who would not die.

For Reflection

If the apostles had difficulty understanding what Jesus was telling them, it's understandable that today's religious leaders too would have difficulty discerning God's will for the Church. Pray that the Holy Spirit will give religious leaders wisdom so they can discern God's will for his people.

3rd Sunday of Lent

John 2:13-25

The only place where the Jews could legitimately offer sacrifices to God was in the Temple in Jerusalem, and they believed they should offer only the finest and healthiest animals as a sacrifice because God deserves the best. Offering anything less was out of the question. Sometimes the priests and unscrupulous merchants used this belief to cheat the poor.

A poor Jewish shepherd picks out the best sheep or goat to take to the Temple as an offering to God. When he arrives at the Temple, the priest inspects the animal and declares it unfit for sacrifice. The shepherd wants to make an offering to God but doesn't have time for the long trip back home to get another animal. Just outside the Temple there are merchants selling animals they guarantee to be fit for sacrifice. However, the cost is greatly inflated because the priest who rejected the original animal will get a commission. As you can guess, there really wasn't anything wrong with the shepherd's sheep or goat. The merchants and the priests were really working together for mutual profit. Reluctantly, the shepherd pays the price, offers the sacrifice, and returns home.

Moneychangers also set up tables in the Temple area because the Jews had to pay a temple tax with Jewish currency. They could not use Roman coins for this purpose because the Romans engraved their coins with the image of the emperor, whom they worshiped as a god. The Jews thought it wouldn't be right to pay the tax to the one true God with a coin bearing the image of a false god.

The moneychangers made huge profits by exchanging the Roman coins for less than they were really worth and using some of the profit to bribe the priests into continuing to allow them to do their business in the Temple precincts. Again, the poor suffered the most from this practice.

Some Jews believed the messiah would purify the Temple. That's exactly what Jesus does in today's Gospel when he turns over the moneychangers' tables and drives out those selling animals in the Temple area. These actions cut into the profits of the priests and the Jewish leaders who later handed Jesus over to the Romans to be killed.

For Reflection

Jesus stuck up for those who were poor and oppressed. Who are the poor and the oppressed in our world today? What are *you* doing during Lent to promote justice for them?

4th Sunday of Lent

John 3:14-21

Although the Romans were in control of Palestine in the time of Christ, they permitted the people they conquered to exercise a limited amount of self rule. The Jews in Palestine did this through the Sanhedrin, the town council in Jerusalem, a combination of our Congress and the Supreme Court but for Jewish religious purposes. The Sanhedrin passed laws and then enforced these laws by arresting and putting on trial anyone accused of breaking them. If the Sanhedrin found the accused guilty, it would then prescribe a punishment for the crime. The only restriction the Romans placed on the Sanhedrin was that it could not carry out the death penalty. That was something the Romans reserved for themselves.

In today's Gospel, a man named Nicodemus, a member of the Sanhedrin, comes to visit Jesus at night. This is interesting because the members of the Sanhedrin later arrested Jesus, found him guilty of blasphemy, decreed that he should die for this offense, and then (because they could not carry out a sentence of capital punishment) sent him to the Roman governor with the charge of treason (which, according to Roman law, was punishable by death).

During their late night conversation, Jesus and Nicodemus talk about a bizarre event recorded in the book of Numbers (21:4-9). After escaping from slavery in Egypt, the Jewish people wandered in the desert for forty years. During that time, they experienced many hardships, and some of them even wondered out loud if they made a mistake by leaving Egypt. As a result of their grumbling and apparent lack of trust in him, God allowed a plague of serpents to afflict them. Many who were bitten by one of these serpents died.

When the people repented of their sin, God told Moses to make a bronze serpent and hold it up in the middle of the camp. Those who had been bitten looked at this bronze serpent and did not die.

In today's Gospel we hear that just as Moses lifted up the serpent in the middle of the camp, so must Jesus, the Son of Man, be lifted up on the cross. The meaning of this analogy is clear. Just as those who looked at the bronze serpent regained their health, those who look to Jesus will receive a spiritual healing resulting in eternal life.

For Reflection

A self-proclaimed minister buys tickets to nationally televised sporting events and attends these events wearing a T-shirt that says, "John 3:16." This minister gets seats or positions himself where the camera is sure to focus so people from coast to coast will see his message. John 3:16 is part of today's Gospel reading. Look up the passage. Why does this minister believe this passage is so important?

5th Sunday of Lent

John 12:20-33

In many Gospel stories, Jesus calls himself "the Son of Man," a title some Jewish people may have associated with the messiah, a military leader who would free them from foreign oppression. To understand the connection between these two terms, let's look at the context in which "the Son of Man" appears in the Old Testament.

"Son of Man" first appears in Daniel 7:13, a verse that is part of a chapter in which the author talks about four great military powers all trying, at different times, to control the world. Because these ruthless and merciless forces put fear in the hearts of anyone who stood in their way, the author uses images of frightening beasts to describe them. Thus, in Daniel 7:1-8 we read about a lion with eagle's wings (Babylonians), a bear with three tusks (Medes), a leopard with four wings and four heads (Persians) and a beast with iron teeth and ten horns (Assyrians).

The author of the book of Daniel tries to give hope to his audience by saying God will one day send a new power to conquer the world, a power that will rule more like a human being (a son of man) than like an animal. Instead of instilling fear, this new power will reign with justice and compassion.

Because each of the animals in Daniel 7:1-8 symbolizes a mighty nation, not an individual, some Jewish people concluded that "the Son of Man" was also symbolic of a nation—the Jewish nation. They believed that one day God will use them to conquer the world and through them God will rule the world like it should be ruled. They called this period of time with God in control the reign or the kingdom of God.

Other Jews realized that their nation could not establish the reign of God all by itself so they believed God would help them by sending someone gifted with the divine spirit to lead them in battle. Thus, Son of Man sometimes referred to an individual rather than a nation.

In today's Gospel, Jesus says it is time for the Son of Man to be glorified. Although he is talking about his own death, many of the Jews understood this to mean the day they were waiting for had finally arrived. The messiah had come into the world and God's reign was about to begin.

For Reflection

Some of the Jewish people believed they were God's instrument for change in the world. Pray this week that you too will be God's instrument so your family and friends can experience his love and forgiveness through you.

Palm Sunday

Mark 14:1-15:47

Because the Gospel for Palm Sunday and Good Friday is always about the crucifixion and death of Jesus, we may benefit from taking a closer look at the details surrounding Jesus' Passion. Therefore, we will focus today on crucifixion in general and will not limit our examination to any one particular Gospel account.

The soldier who scourged Jesus before he was crucified used a short wooden handled instrument called a flagrum made from fragments of bone or metal tied to three strips of leather. According to Roman law, a criminal could not be scourged more than forty times because he might die from too severe a beating. As a precaution against accidental over-scourging, the Romans usually administered only thirty-nine lashes.

The Gospels also tell us Jesus carried his cross to the place where the soldiers crucified him but they do not give us any details about what the cross actually looked like. Although we usually picture Jesus dragging the entire cross behind him, he probably carried only the crossbeam on which the soldiers later nailed his hands. Because the crossbeam alone weighed about 125 pounds, the entire cross would have been much too heavy for one man to carry.

Another misconception is that the soldiers drove the nails through the palms of Jesus' hands. Scientists tell us the palms could not possibly have supported the weight of the body because the flesh would have torn and the body would have fallen from the cross. Therefore, the soldiers most likely drove each nail through the wrist at a point where it separated two bones, thus providing an anchor for the nail and preventing the flesh from tearing and the body from falling.

Death usually came because the convicted criminal could not expel air from his lungs. With arms outstretched on the cross, the victim was able to inhale but not exhale. Therefore, the Romans often nailed a little step at the foot of the cross so the victim could push his body upward and into a position in which he could exhale. When the Romans wanted to speed up the entire crucifixion process, they'd break the criminal's legs so he could not push his body upward. With lungs fully expanded, he'd soon die of asphyxiation.

For Reflection

Jesus was wrongly accused and punished for crimes he did not commit. Pray this week that judges and juries may have the wisdom to make just and true decisions. Pray also for innocent people who are serving time in jail.

Please refer to Cycle A for the following commentaries:

Easter . . . . page 32

Pentecost . . . . page 46

2nd Sunday of Easter

John 20:19-31

The apostle Thomas is one of the main characters in today's Gospel, but the picture the author paints of him is not very flattering. In this reading, Thomas refuses to believe Jesus is alive unless he can first put his fingers into the nail marks in Jesus' hands and examine the wound in Jesus' side. Because of Thomas' need to see before believing, we sometimes call him and any other skeptic "Doubting Thomas."

If we put ourselves in Thomas' place and if we are honest about how we would have responded in the same situation, we probably wouldn't judge him as harshly as we sometimes do. Thomas had seen Jesus crucified and was sure Jesus had died. He talked to the women who stood at the foot of the cross and maybe even spoke to the men who took Jesus' body and laid it in the tomb. Jesus was dead and there was no doubt about it.

Thomas wanted to believe Jesus was alive, but how could it be possible? No, the disciples were only dreaming, he must have thought. Overcome with grief, they were not being rational. They did not want to admit Jesus was dead, so they convinced themselves the whole thing never occurred. Thomas wanted no part of this charade.

Can you imagine how Thomas felt when he finally did see the resurrected Jesus? Can you picture how stunned he was? Dead men do not come back to life, but here was the same Jesus Thomas was sure had been crucified and buried. The others were not dreaming. Jesus was alive! He had risen from the dead!

Thomas had his faults but he also had some virtues. In John 11, the disciples tried to convince Jesus not to go to Judea because some of the Jews there wanted to stone him. When it was clear Jesus would not change his mind, Thomas said to the other apostles that he was willing to go along with Jesus to die (verse 16). It appears Thomas was a pretty gutsy guy.

Today's Gospel also testifies to Thomas' courage. The apostles locked themselves in the upper room because they were afraid the Romans would crucify them just as they crucified Jesus. Only Thomas had enough nerve to venture outside.

We don't know much more about Thomas because Scripture doesn't say much about him. However, tradition tells us he became a missionary to India and preached the Gospel there until he died for his faith. In the end, no one could doubt Thomas' faith and courage.

For Reflection

Pretend you are Thomas. The resurrected Jesus appears to you and tells you he will answer any question you might have. What question would you ask him?

3rd Sunday of Easter

Luke 24:35-48

In today's Gospel Jesus tells his disciples to preach penance for the remission of sins. Many of us think of penance as something old fashioned our parents or grandparents did a long time ago, not as something we do today. Before we cast aside this ancient spiritual practice, however, we first should take a better look at what it really is and how it fits into our spiritual lives.

I'm sure you've heard the expression "I'd give my right arm if I could only have _____ (fill in the blank)," an expression that means I want something so much I am willing to suffer for it if I have to. If I am not willing to suffer for something, then it's doubtful I really value it. We can use this same reasoning when we talk about doing penance for our sins.

Jesus encourages us to do penance as a way of telling God we really want his forgiveness. Thus, penance is a way we communicate to God that his forgiveness is so important to us we are even willing to sacrifice or suffer for it. However, we must always remember that forgiveness comes from Jesus, not from something we do.

In the past, we associated penance with giving something up, especially food. Until recently, Catholics fasted and abstained from meat each Friday (the day of the week Jesus died on the cross) as a sign they really did want God to forgive them. A problem arose when they sometimes forgot why they were fasting and did it only because it was church law.

Another thing we need to remember is that penance is not always giving up something. It also may involve visiting a sick friend or shopping for an elderly neighbor. It might mean spending a little extra time in prayer or attending church services on a weekday. Whatever the penance is, we can be sure it will get God's attention.

For Reflection

Make a list of some of the ways you can do penance. From this list choose one thing you will do this week to show God you really value his forgiveness.

4th Sunday of Easter

John 10:11-18

Sheep herding was one of the three main occupations in Jesus' time because sheep provided so many useful items, including milk, meat, hides (for making clothing and tent coverings), and wool. Ancient people even used the horns as musical instruments and as containers for oil.

Sheep were totally dependent on the shepherd and a very close relationship developed between them and him. The shepherd even gave each of the sheep names and they responded when he called because they recognized his voice. Since sheep often wandered from the flock, the shepherd had to count his sheep several times a day and, if he discovered one missing, he left the rest of the sheep with another shepherd and went to look for the stray. The shepherd also took care of pregnant ewes that went into labor and nursed sick sheep back to health.

Shepherding not only lacked glamour, but it also didn't pay very well. Many people often stereotyped shepherds as thieves because, they reasoned, the shepherds had to steal in order to survive on their pay. The shepherd's working conditions were also terrible because when the sheep were grazing far away from home the shepherd had to sleep out in the open, fully exposed to the elements of nature.

A shepherd's job was also dangerous because he had to be constantly on the lookout for wild animals and thieves who threatened the flock. The shepherd defended his sheep and was even willing to give his life for them if that became necessary.

In today's Gospel, Jesus calls himself the Good Shepherd and he says we are his sheep. Like a shepherd, Jesus leads us and protects us, giving extra attention to the weak and to those who have special needs. When Jesus notices one of his sheep has strayed, he searches until he finds it and returns home rejoicing with the errant sheep on his shoulders. Like a good shepherd, Jesus even gave his life in defense of his flock.

Perhaps what is even more important is the loving relationship between the shepherd and his sheep. Nothing else could possibly explain the shepherd's willingness to expose himself to such harsh conditions and extreme danger. Being our Good Shepherd, Jesus wants to have that same kind of close and loving relationship with each of us.

For Reflection

Jesus compared himself to a good shepherd because shepherding was one of the main occupations of the people to whom he preached. If Jesus appeared today instead of 2,000 years ago, what modern occupation would he compare his ministry to?

5th Sunday of Easter

Jesus was a successful preacher because he often talked about topics familiar to the people of his day. Today's Gospel reading is a good example. Grape vines were plentiful in first-century Palestine and grapes were one of the most important crops at that time, sometimes eaten right off the vine and sometimes dried into raisins or made into wine (the most common drink at a meal in Jesus' day).

Growing grapes was a lot of work. The vinegrower first prepared the soil by removing all sticks and stones and then either planting a hedge of prickly plants around the field or building a fence of stones to keep out all animals that might destroy the crop. He then constructed a watchtower so a guard could keep watch over the crop and protect it from mischievous enemies. Finally, he built a wine press and vat so he could make wine from the grapes.

Once planted, the vines grew quickly and the vinegrower had to train them on trellises, sides of houses, or on trees. He pruned the vines regularly and trimmed away branches that did not bear fruit so they would not needlessly drain the vine of water and nutrients. Because the wood of the vine was useless, the vinedresser usually burned all the pruned branches.

In today's Gospel, Jesus says he is the vine and we are the branches. This means that just as the branches depend on the vine for physical life and nourishment, we depend on Jesus for our spiritual life and nourishment.

We are fruitful branches if we make Jesus' love and presence known to those around us by visiting the lonely, feeding the hungry, and clothing the naked. We do so because that's what being a follower of Jesus is all about and because Jesus is the source of our life and strength.

The non-productive branches, those that do not bear fruit, are people who live their lives only for themselves, not for others. These people will wither and die because the vinedresser will prune them away so they are no longer drawing life and nutrients from the vine. Just as no branch can survive without the vine, neither can we survive spiritually without Jesus.

For Reflection

What are some of the bad habits you have to prune out of your life so you can be a more productive Christian? Pray this week that Jesus will help you be a more fruitful branch.

6th Sunday of Easter

John 15:9-17

The Bible often pictures God as a groom who jealously loves and cares for his bride (his chosen people), and time after time it compares God's love for us to the love between a husband and wife. This intense love relationship is what makes the Christian God different from the gods of most other religions. Some religions teach about a God who, because he is other-worldly and distant, is not concerned about our everyday lives; other religions teach about a powerful God or a vengeful and punishing God. Along with Judaism and Islam, Christianity is one of the few religions that teaches about a God of love who is not only interested in us but who also wants to share his life with us.

Two people who love each other try to make each other happy. A husband shows love for his wife by doing the things that please her and by avoiding the things that make her angry. The wife, likewise, shows her love for her husband in the same manner. However, they first have to communicate what it is that pleases them. They need to make their likes and dislikes known to each other, telling each other how to love. This same process takes place in our relationship with God.

In today's reading, Jesus tells us we can show our love for him by keeping his commandments. This means we shouldn't think of the commandments just as a list of do's and don'ts but rather compare them to the husband who buys his wife flowers on her birthday or the wife who surprises her husband by baking his favorite pie. Just as these are ways a married couple says "I love you" to each other, following the commandments are ways we can say "I love you" to God.

As in other relationships, our relationship with God is a two way street. We not only show our love for God but God also shows his love for us. Jesus showed the depth of his love by dying on the cross for us, a love so great he was even willing to suffer pain and endure humiliation on our behalf. As Jesus says in today's Gospel, the greatest love possible is for a person to give his life for his friends. We are Jesus' friends if we do what he commands us.

For Reflection

Friends like to spend time together. Take ten minutes today to go someplace by yourself so you can spend some quiet time with your friend Jesus. Sit in a comfortable chair and relax. Forget about whatever is bothering you and simply be aware of Jesus' presence. Do this for a few minutes each day and see the difference it makes.

7th Sunday of Easter

John 17:11-19

The Church divides its calendar of Sunday readings into three parts called cycles, with a new cycle beginning on the first Sunday of Advent. The Church takes the cycle A Sunday Gospel readings from the Gospel according to Matthew, the cycle B Gospel readings from the Gospel according to Mark, and the cycle C Gospel readings from the Gospel according to Luke. John's Gospel is part of all three cycles, usually appearing on special occasions such as Holy Thursday, Good Friday, and the Sundays during the Easter season. Most of the Sunday Gospel readings so far this year have been from the Gospel according to Mark because we are in the middle of the B cycle of readings.

One unusual feature in the Gospel according to John is that it uses the term "disciples" rather than "apostles." Sometimes priests and ministers use these two words interchangeably as if they mean the same thing. In reality, they have very different definitions.

Jesus' followers often addressed him as "Rabbi," a word that means "teacher." The word "disciple" comes from a Greek word that means "student." Some rabbis taught Jewish boys how to read and write in the synagogue schools, but other rabbis taught men how to be rabbis. In either case, the rabbi's students were his

158

disciples. Therefore, John is correct when he uses this word to describe the twelve men whom Jesus chose to be his close companions because they were his students, training to become rabbis.

The word "apostle" comes from a Greek word that means "one who is sent," and it refers to someone who is sent out to deliver a message. Matthew, Mark, and Luke call the twelve men whom Jesus chose to be his close companions "apostles" because Jesus sent them out to proclaim the Gospel message after he taught them privately. In other words, they were disciples or students first and were apostles after they successfully completed their period of instruction.

It is interesting that we do not find the word "apostle" in the Gospel according to John. The closest John comes to using this word is in today's reading when Jesus, in his prayer to his heavenly Father, says he "sent" the Twelve out into the world. For John, the true follower of Jesus never stops being a disciple but is always willing to learn more about Jesus and his message.

For Reflection

What kind of disciple are you? How much time do you spend reading and studying Scripture so Jesus can use you as his apostle in the world today?

2nd Sunday in Ordinary Time

John 1:35-42

In today's Gospel reading, two of John the Baptist's disciples address Jesus as "Rabbi," which means "teacher." In those days, a rabbi was the most educated person in a city or town and because he was usually the only one who could read or write fluently, the people paid him a great deal of respect.

There were two types of rabbis in Jesus' day. The first type used the Sacred Scripture to teach Jewish boys how to read and write in the synagogue school. These boys were preparing for the day when they would become adults in their faith, obligated to following all of the Jewish laws.

The second type of rabbi, a master rabbi, taught other men how to be rabbis and provided his disciples with food and shelter while he instructed them. The disciples, in turn, worked for the master rabbi. Jesus was this type of rabbi.

Because both types of rabbis were knowledgeable about the Sacred Scripture and because that's where the Jewish laws are, the townspeople consulted the rabbis whenever they had a question about how they should interpret a particular law. Sometimes, lively public debates took place when two or more rabbis offered different opinions. Since there are many examples of people coming to Jesus seeking his advice, we can conclude that Jesus also engaged in public debates with the other rabbis of his day.

The rabbi was not the Jewish version of a priest or minister. Rabbis did not (and still do not) lead the synagogue services, and they did not offer sacrifices in the Temple. Rather, teaching was their main function.

For Reflection

Religious education was very important to the Jewish people who lived in Jesus' day. It was a lifelong pursuit and not something only children engage in. When was the last time you attended a religious education class so your knowledge of your faith would grow? Pray this week for catechists and other religious educators who teach in your parish.

3rd Sunday in Ordinary Time

Mark 1:14-20

Since Jesus lived near the Sea of Galilee, a fishing hot spot of the ancient world, he had many friends and acquaintances who were fishermen. Some of the twelve apostles, too, fished for a living.

Because fish was the main source of protein for the people of Palestine, fishing was one of the most common ways of earning a living in New Testament times. Jesus sometimes got the attention of the many fishermen in his audience by relating parables with familiar images. For instance, Jesus once compared the reign of God to a net thrown into the sea (Matthew 13:47-50). This parable and others like it interested the fishermen who came to hear Jesus preach.

Some of our most popular Church symbols came from the fishing experience of the early Christians. One such symbol, a fish, was popular because the first letters of the Greek words "Jesus Christ, God's Son, Savior" (*iesous christos theou huios soter*) spell out the Greek word for fish. This symbol played a very important role in the growth of the Church.

Because the Roman authorities often put Christians to death for their faith, Christians had to take precautions so a spy would not come to one of their meetings, find out who all the Christians were, and then turn them in for a reward. Therefore, a person who desired baptism first had to contact someone he thought was a Christian. While talking, this person would use a toe to draw half a fish in the sand. If the other person was indeed a Christian, this individual would complete the drawing as a sign it was safe to speak freely. The Christian would introduce the new person to the rest of the community of believers only after determining the individual was not a spy.

Because part of an anchor formed the shape of a cross, it also became a popular Christian symbol. The early followers of Jesus often attached an anchor to the outside door of the house where they were celebrating the Eucharist so other Christians could more easily find the place where they were meeting.

For Reflection

Jesus took advantage of the fishing skills of the apostles to do such things as sail across the sea instead of walking around it. What skills do you possess that Jesus can use to make his Gospel known today?

4th Sunday in Ordinary Time

Mark 1:21-28

Ancient people did not know about germs and viruses because they did not have all the benefits of modern medicine. Therefore, ancient explanations of how people got sick and why people died may sound a little simplistic or naive to us. Most people, including the Jews, attributed sickness and death to the power of demons or evil spirits.

Jesus began his preaching by proclaiming the reign of God is at hand. This meant that because God was about to defeat the devil and take control of the world, the signs of the devil's power (sickness and death) would be only memories of the past.

Today's Gospel reading is a dramatic example of the struggle between Jesus and the devil. Jesus is in the synagogue preaching when a man with an unclean spirit yells out, calling Jesus by name and identifying him as God's Holy One.

In Scripture, the power to name someone is symbolic of having control over that person. In the second chapter of Genesis, God brought the animals he created to the man and the man named them, symbolizing his dominion over them.

The second commandment says we must not take the name of God in vain. The Jews understood this to mean they should not use God's name at all because doing so was like trying to exert power over God. Therefore, God would have to act if his name is used in a curse and he would have to damn that person.

Similarly, the unclean spirit in today's Gospel tries to exert power over Jesus by calling him first by name and then by referring to him as the Holy One sent by God, a title for the messiah. Fortunately for the man who was possessed, this tactic doesn't work and Jesus shows he is more powerful than the devil by commanding him to get out of the man. However, the battle does not end there because the demon does not obey without putting up a struggle. First, he throws the man into convulsions and only then does he come out with a loud shriek. Finally, the battle is over and Jesus wins.

For Reflection

The battle between Jesus and the devil continues even today. Each day of our lives we have to make decisions. Pray for the grace to always decide to do God's will so that his reign will grow.

5th Sunday in Ordinary Time

Mark 1:29-39

In excavations of the city of Capernaum, archaeologists have found the remains of a first-century synagogue, probably the same synagogue Jesus preached in. They also found a fifth-century octagon-shaped church next to the synagogue (fifth-century Christians often built octagon churches to mark important religious landmarks) and two other buildings under the church, one of which is a house that dates back to Jesus' day. Inscriptions on the walls of this house identify it as the home of Simon Peter, the apostle; it is probably the same house we hear about in today's Gospel.

Today's Gospel ends by telling us Jesus preached the good news in the synagogues and he expelled demons. Preaching and healing were two important parts of Jesus' ministry.

Jesus' message was that the reign of God is here, which meant the messiah, through whom God would establish his kingdom, had come into the world. Some of the Jews of Jesus' time expected this messiah to be a political/military leader who would defeat their human enemies. That was their big mistake. Jesus was indeed a military leader, but the battle he fought was not against human adversaries but against a powerful spiritual foe, the devil himself.

Since many ancient people believed demons and evil spirits caused sickness and disease, every time Jesus healed someone it meant he was defeating the devil. Each miracle, then, was a visible sign Jesus was winning his battle against the devil and God was retaking control of the world. Thus, the reign of God Jesus was preaching about was becoming a reality.

In 1 Corinthians 12:27, when St. Paul says the Church is the Body of Christ and we are the members of that Body, he means Jesus continues to do the things today that he did 2,000 years ago with his physical body. He does these things through you and me because we are his hands and feet and his eyes and ears. Jesus uses us as his instruments to continue defeating the devil and making the reign of God grow.

Being part of the Body of Christ means Jesus preaches and heals through you and me. He preaches through us when we share our faith with each other and with our children. Jesus heals through us when we visit the elderly neighbor who suffers from the pain of loneliness and when we support soup kitchens or relief agencies. Therefore, Jesus is still very active in the world and continues to defeat the devil and retake control of the world even today.

For Reflection

Being part of the Body of Christ means we have a responsibility to preach and heal. Make a list of the ways Jesus preaches and heals through you. These are the ways Jesus uses you to make the reign of God grow.

6th Sunday in Ordinary Time

Mark 1:40-45

Leprosy in biblical times was not the dreaded disease we know by that name today but was any white, crusty patch on a person's skin. The people in Jesus' day considered eczema and skin diseases like it to be leprosy.

According to the Jewish faith, lepers were ritually unclean. This did not mean they were sinful or dirty but that they could not worship in the Temple or offer sacrifices there. Lepers also lived outside the city walls and cried out "unclean, unclean" whenever someone came near them. Anyone who touched a leper was also unclean.

Because leprosy prevented the person from associating with others, especially in public worship, today's first reading instructs the leper to rend or tear a piece of clothing, an ancient Jewish sign of grief.

A person who recovered from the leprosy first met a priest outside the city walls and if the priest found the leprosy had indeed cleared up, the leper would take a ritual bath and then offer certain sacrifices to God. The type of sacrifice depended on the person's financial ability. Only after washing and offering the sacrifices could the person return to the city and worship with the rest of the community.

Notice that in today's Gospel reading Jesus not only associates with the leper but he also does something the ordinary person would not dare do. Jesus stretches out his hand and actually touches the man, healing him on the spot. Jesus then instructs him to show himself to the priest and to offer the appropriate sacrifices in the Temple.

Notice also that Jesus tells the man not to say anything to anyone about being healed. We find this messianic secret, as biblical scholars call it, only in the Gospel according to Mark. In no other Gospel does Jesus perform a miracle and then instruct the person not to make the incident public. Scripture scholars do not know why Jesus does this or why the same or similar stories in the other Gospels do not contain this detail.

For Reflection

Lepers were the people society shunned in Jesus' day. Who are the outcasts in our own society today? How would Jesus want us to treat these people?

7th Sunday in Ordinary Time

Mark 2:1-12

Most of us know Jesus was born in Bethlehem and grew up in Nazareth, but very few people are able to identify where Jesus lived as an adult. Because today's Gospel tells us Jesus went "back home" to Capernaum, a town on the northwest shore of the sea of Galilee, it is logical to conclude that Jesus lived there during his public ministry.

In Jesus' day, wealthy people built homes in the shape of the letter U, with a courtyard in the middle. An outside staircase leading up to a flat roof was an important feature of most houses because people often used their roof for drying grains and fruit. The men who carried the paralytic in today's Gospel reading used this staircase to get him onto the roof and were then able to make a hole through which they could lower him into the house because the roof was made of mud and straw pressed between wooden rafters.

A controversy arises when Jesus tells the paralyzed man his sins are forgiven. Since the Pharisees taught that only God could forgive sins, they object to Jesus claiming he too has that power and they even accuse him of blasphemy (being irreverent to God).

Jesus responds by asking the Pharisees if it is easier to tell the paralyzed man to get up and walk or to tell him his sins are forgiven. Anybody could claim to have power to forgive sins because no one would be able to prove otherwise but claiming to have the ability to heal the sick is much more difficult because skeptics would demand a demonstration.

Jesus' reasoning is clear. If he is able to do the more difficult of the two, then that should be proof he is also able to do that which is easier. To use a modern example, if I can multiply, I am also able to add. However, being able to add does not mean I know how to multiply. Therefore, what Jesus is saying is that, because it is the more difficult to do, being able to make the man walk should serve as proof that he is also able to forgive sins.

The connection between Jesus healing and forgiving sins is even clearer considering that the Pharisees taught that sickness resulted either because of one's own sin or because of a sin committed by one's parents. Therefore, according to this teaching, Jesus would not have been able to heal the man unless he first forgave the man's sins.

For Reflection

When was the last time you asked God to forgive your sins? Do you really believe God forgives?

8th Sunday in Ordinary Time

Mark 2:18-22

The Pharisees in first-century Palestine fasted twice a week. On those days (usually Mondays and Thursdays), they put ashes on their head and didn't comb their hair or trim their beard, all actions symbolic of penance and sorrow. They then stood on street corners so others, noticing how often they performed acts of penance, would conclude they were holy.

In today's Gospel, the Pharisees ask Jesus why the apostles didn't fast like they did. Jesus' response sounds strange because, instead of answering the question, he begins talking about weddings, mending garments, and filling wineskins. What does all this have to do with fasting? A modern example may help us understand Jesus' response.

Sometimes people will answer a question with another question. For instance, if you ask someone if they are going to the movies, they may respond by saying "Is the pope Catholic?" The answer to one question is also the answer to the other question. Yes, the pope is Catholic. Yes, I am going to the movies. The two questions have nothing to do with each other except that they share the same answer. Jesus used this same technique in today's Gospel.

A wedding is a happy occasion but fasting is a sign of sorrow. Would a person fast during a wedding feast? Of course not! That wouldn't make much sense.

In the days before preshrunk material, a person had to wash a patch before using it to cover a hole on an old garment. If the patch was sewed on before the garment was washed, the patch would shrink but the garment wouldn't, causing the patch to pull away and making the hole bigger. Therefore, it wouldn't make sense to sew a new patch on an old garment.

Finally, Jesus talks about putting new wine into old skins. Since glass bottles were rare and expensive, people stored wine in animal skins folded in half and sewn into a pouch. Because new wine fermenting in the skins caused expansion, they did not store new wine in old skins already stretched to their limit. If they did, the skins would stretch more and burst.

Jesus' answer means that just as it does not make sense to do any of these things, it doesn't make sense to perform acts of penance just to impress others. Like all these other things, fasting for show should not be done.

For Reflection

Jesus objected not to fasting but to doing it for show. Fasting shows God that we really want something and are willing to sacrifice for it. If we're not willing to do that, we probably don't really want it. In their pastoral letter on peace, the American Catholic bishops suggest we fast once a week for world peace.

9th Sunday in Ordinary Time

Mark 2:23-3:6

The Pharisees had such great respect for the laws in Sacred Scripture they were almost paranoid about even accidentally breaking one of them. Therefore, they created other laws to guarantee the laws in scripture would not be broken. The Pharisees called these man-made laws the oral traditions because they believed these laws were handed down from generation to generation beginning with Moses himself.

The oral traditions spelled out precisely what an individual could and could not do on the Sabbath. For instance, they said a person could not cook a meal, light a candle, or walk more than a certain distance. The oral traditions even went so far as to say a doctor could not treat a sick person on the Sabbath if the sickness did not threaten the patient's life.

In today's Gospel, the Pharisees object to the apostles plucking heads of grain on the Sabbath because that was harvesting a crop, an action the oral traditions prohibited. They also object to Jesus' Sabbath healing of a man with a deformed hand because the man's life is not in danger.

Jesus responds by reminding the Pharisees of something David, the great king of the Jews, once did.

While fleeing for his life, David and his men asked the priest of Nob for some food because they were hungry. However, the only food available was the twelve loaves of bread on the table before the tabernacle. This bread was an offering to God and normally stayed on the table for a full week before the priests consumed it. Because they were hungry, David and his men ate the bread only the priests were supposed to eat. The point of the story is that human life is more important than any laws, even religious laws.

In response to the Pharisee's objection about healing the man with the withered hand, Jesus' defense centers on the principle that any law could be broken in order to save a life, a principle even the Pharisees accepted. Jesus went one step further by reasoning that this exception is permissible because saving a life is something good. Therefore, Jesus concludes, if doing a good deed makes it acceptable to break one of the oral traditions, there should be nothing wrong if, on the Sabbath, he heals the man's deformed hand.

For Reflection

Jesus clearly believed people are more important than laws. Is there anything in your life more important than the people around you?

10th Sunday in Ordinary Time

Mark 3:20-35

In today's Gospel, the scribes accuse Jesus of casting out demons with the help of Beelzebul, the prince of demons. Beelzebul is a form of Baal, the Canaanite god of weather who controlled the forces of nature (like thunderstorms, wind, rain, etc.). The Canaanites believed Baal sent rain and sun to make the crops grow if he was happy but destroyed the crops with drought, flood, or some other natural catastrophe if he was upset.

Baal was also the god of fertility and, because he cavorted with the goddess Astarte, temple prostitutes were part of the pagan worship ritual in his honor. To please Baal and Astarte, someone would imitate them by sleeping with the temple prostitute. It's easy to understand why Baal became a very popular god.

The Jewish people were introduced to Baal worship by their pagan neighbors. The prophets and Jewish leaders warned the Jews about the dangers of worshiping this false god but many of them gave up their faith in the one true God anyway. Faithful Jews, however, ridiculed Baal worship by first changing the god's name to Baalzebub meaning "lord of the flies" and then Baalzebul meaning "lord of dung." Eventually, Baalzebul became Beelzebul, the name in today's Gospel. By Jesus' day, the Jews pictured Beelzebul as the very powerful prince of demons.

Ignorant about germs and bacteria, the people in biblical times believed demons caused sickness. Therefore, they interpreted Jesus' healing miracles as exorcisms of these demons. The scribes in today's Gospel reason that Jesus gets his power to expel demons from Beelzebul, the prince of demons. This accusation didn't make much sense because it means Beelzebul was fighting against his own troops and, if this were so, his kingdom could not last.

The Gospel story ends with a surprising and shocking statement. Most people believe God will forgive all sins, no matter what they might be. However, Jesus said one sin, the sin of blasphemy against the Holy Spirit, could not be forgiven. Although biblical scholars aren't sure what this sin is, some suggest it may be when a person says the Holy Spirit's power comes from the devil. This would be like saying God is the devil and, since the devil does not forgive sins, forgiveness would not be possible.

For Reflection

Some people think witnessing a miracle would make their faith in Jesus stronger. However, there were many people who witnessed Jesus making the blind see, the deaf hear, and the lame walk and still did not believe in him. Faith sometimes leads to miracles but miracles do not always lead to faith. Pray today for greater faith for yourself and your family.

11th Sunday in Ordinary Time

Mark 4:26-34

People are naturally reluctant to change their minds about traditional beliefs and the Jewish people in Jesus' day were no different from anyone else. They, too, were set in their ways and were reluctant to abandon their long held convictions, especially religious doctrines pertaining to the messiah.

Some Jewish people in first-century Palestine believed the messiah would conquer the world and, through him, God would then restore the world to what it was like before man and woman sinned. This is what the Jews called the reign or kingdom of God.

Some Jews believed the reign of God would come quickly once the messiah appeared and that it would be only for the Jewish people. Jesus challenges these ideas with the parables in today's Gospel.

Jesus compares the reign of God to a seed and in the first parable, he stresses how slowly a seed grows. First there's the blade, then the ear, and finally the ripe wheat in the ear. Just as this process takes time and doesn't occur overnight, the reign of God will also take time and will not happen all at once.

In the second parable, Jesus says that the reign of God is like a mustard seed that grows into a huge plant in which the birds of the air build their nests. Notice that Jesus does not say the birds were only sparrows, or only robins, or only blue jays. Just as all birds build their nests in the tree, the reign of God will be for all people, not only for the Jews.

Knowing the people in his audience were likely to cling stubbornly to their cherished beliefs, Jesus usually chose not to come right out and tell them they were wrong. That method wouldn't succeed. Instead, Jesus used parables because he knew people were more likely to remember them and share them with family and friends, discussing the meaning of each parable as they did so. In this way Jesus got them to re-examine their traditional beliefs and challenged them to think in a new direction without threatening them.

For Reflection

Each time we pray the Our Father, we pray for God's kingdom to come. We pray for the day when God will conquer the devil and restore the world to what it was like before man and woman sinned. In today's Gospel, Jesus tells us to be patient. He will defeat the devil, but it will take time.

12th Sunday in Ordinary Time

Mark 4:35-41

Today's Gospel takes place on the Sea of Galilee, one of the fishing hot spots of the ancient world because it was the home of over forty different species of fish. Fishermen returning from a hard day's work brought their catch ashore and smoked the fish to prevent spoiling (there weren't any refrigerators in those days) before shipping them to distant parts of the Roman empire.

In today's Gospel, Jesus and some of the apostles are in a boat on the Sea of Galilee when they get caught in the middle of a fierce storm. Since some of the apostles were fishermen, you would think they would have had enough common sense not to get into a boat when it was obvious that a storm was brewing. This may be a reasonable assumption when talking about most lakes but the Sea of Galilee presents some special problems.

Hills as high as 1,200-1,500 feet surround this particular body of water and fierce winds sometimes whip around these hills, picking up speed in whirlwind fashion and causing strong gusts that churn up the water and threaten small boats. Because these storms come suddenly without much warning and end just as abruptly, there was probably no way the apostles could have anticipated unfavorable sailing conditions.

The miraculous event in today's Gospel is more than just a demonstration of Jesus' power over the forces of nature. It also has a deeper, spiritual meaning we should not overlook.

In the Old Testament, the biblical authors often used a body of water to symbolize the dwelling place of devils or evil spirits and wind to symbolize their power. Therefore, by rebuking the wind and calming the sea Jesus demonstrates that he is more powerful than the devil. Jesus meets the devil on the devil's own territory and is victorious. The real significance of this miracle, then, is not that Jesus has power over the forces of nature but that he conquers the forces of sin and evil.

For Reflection

The apostles did all they could on their own but were powerless without Jesus. Because we, too, are helpless by ourselves, we should not wait until we are in trouble before calling on him. We should get in the habit of making Jesus part of *everything* we do (not just our problems), and he will not disappoint us.

13th Sunday in Ordinary Time

Mark 5:21-43

Today's Gospel reading contains two very different miracle stories. In one, a woman suffering from a hemorrhage experiences a healing when she touches Jesus' clothing and, in the other, Jesus brings a twelve year old girl back to life. As different as these two miracle are, they do have one thing in common. Each miracle required faith.

Having touched Jesus, the woman feels she has been healed. Being aware that healing power has gone from him, Jesus turns around and asks who touched him. After the woman admits she is the one, Jesus says she has been healed because of her faith. She didn't regain her health because of what she did but because she believed in Jesus' power to heal her.

Something similar happens in the story about Jesus bringing the little girl back to life. When the messengers from the synagogue official's house bring word that the girl is dead, Jesus responds by telling them that fear is useless and that they need to learn to trust (have faith) in him.

When he arrives at the synagogue official's house, Jesus hears people crying and carrying on because, according to custom, the family probably hired professional mourners to help them express their grief. Flute players usually accompanied these professional mourners because ancient people associated the flute's ominous sound with death and tragedy.

Another Jewish mourning custom involved tearing a piece of one's clothing upon hearing the news of the death of a friend or relative. The tear was on the left side when the deceased was one's parent and on the right side for everyone else. The Jews believed this expression of grief was an outward and visible sign of the damage death did to the mourner's relationship with the deceased. Just as the piece of clothing would never be the same again, the mourner's life also could never be as it was before the person died. Hassidic and Orthodox Jews continue this practice even today.

The Gospel story ends when Jesus enters the room where the little girl is lying and tells her to get up. She immediately stands up and walks around. Faith again makes a miracle possible.

For Reflection

In the Gospels, there is only one example of Jesus not being able to perform a miracle. Look up the story in Mark 6:1-6. What reason does Mark give for Jesus' inability to heal in this instance?

14th Sunday in Ordinary Time

Mark 6:1-6

Because people did not have family names in Jesus' day, there were three different ways one could distinguish two people who had the same name.

First of all, a common designation was where the person lived. Simon of Cyrene, Joseph of Arimathea, and Mary of Magdala are good examples. A problem occurred, however, if the two people with the same name came from the same place.

In that case, friends and acquaintances may have identified the person by occupation. Simon the fisherman, Joseph the carpenter, and Levi the tax collector are just a few examples. Modern last names such as Baker, Smith, and Cook originated in this way.

Finally, ancient people sometimes distinguished a person by who his father was. One of the apostles was James, the son of Zebedee, and another was James, the son of Alphaeus. This custom also found its way into different foreign languages and led to modern last names such as Janowicz, which is Polish for "son of John," and Fitzgerald, which is Irish for "son of Gerald." Thus, those who knew Jesus called him Jesus of Nazareth (where he grew up), Jesus of Capernaum (where he lived during his public ministry), Jesus the carpenter, Jesus the rabbi, or Jesus the son of Joseph. Any one of these names would have been appropriate.

Jesus left Nazareth as a simple carpenter but he returned as a famous rabbi with his own disciples. People throughout Palestine heard of his reputation and respected him but the people in his home town gave him a lukewarm reception.

In today's Gospel, the people of Nazareth marvel at Jesus' ability to preach and they ask one another if he isn't the carpenter and the son of Mary. Notice that they do not call Jesus the son of Joseph. Either Joseph was already dead or they meant this as an insult. By not recognizing Joseph as the father of Jesus, they may have been implying he was an illegitimate child. In modern slang, they were calling Jesus a bastard. Therefore, Jesus' homecoming was less than a big success.

For Reflection

It's easy for us to remember that Jesus is God but difficult to think of him as also human. Jesus did not walk around with a neon sign on his chest flashing the words "Worship me, I'm God!" Jesus was just as human as you and I are, and he sometimes experienced what it is like to be hurt and rejected. The next time you feel down, go to Jesus with your problems. He knows what you are going through because he went through the same thing himself.

15th Sunday in Ordinary Time

Mark 6:7-13

The story in today's Gospel begins with Jesus sending the apostles out in pairs to preach and to heal. There were probably two reasons why Jesus did not want the apostles to go out alone.

Cities were far apart and a person going from one city to the next journeyed over long stretches of desert roads that were not heavily traveled. This meant that anyone foolish enough to embark on a journey by himself was an easy prey for the many gangs waiting in ambush to rob and beat those who came along.

There was also a Jewish law which said a judge could not find an accused person guilty if there was only one witness to the alleged offense. The purpose of this law was to protect an innocent person from a neighbor or acquaintance who might make up a story for revenge or blackmail. Therefore, under no circumstances could a judge consider the testimony of only one person sufficient.

The Jews applied the above mentioned law not only in cases involving someone's guilt or innocence, but also in other everyday matters as well. If Jesus had sent out the apostles individually to testify that the reign of God was indeed here, they would have covered twice as many cities but the people who heard them could have challenged their testimony because the required second witness would not have been present. They would have questioned if what the apostles were saying was fact or fiction. By going out in pairs, the apostles verified each other's testimony and those who heard would have accepted it as the truth.

The Gospel story ends with the apostles expelling demons and anointing the sick with oil. Ancient people used oil as a symbol of healing and strength. Athletes rubbed it all over their bodies before competing in sporting events and doctors prescribed it for a variety of illnesses. Today, many Christian denominations continue to use blessed oil for sacraments and prayer. This oil is symbolic of the spiritual strength and the spiritual healing Jesus gives us through the Christian community in our time of need.

For Reflection

Jesus told the apostles not to stay where they were not welcome. Do those who visit your church feel welcome by your parish community? How can you make them feel more at home?

16th Sunday in Ordinary Time

Mark 6:30-34

The Gospel according to Mark contains fewer of Jesus' parables than the other three Gospels. Because Mark seems to have more interest in Jesus' actions than in his teachings, he portrays Jesus as always on the move but records few of his words.

Jesus' humanity expressed through different emotions is another of this Gospel's characteristics. From Mark, we learn Jesus felt anger (11:15-18), irritation (9:19, 14:37), fear (14:33), and compassion (in today's Gospel). Mark sometimes goes out of his way to stress that Jesus experienced the same emotions you and I encounter every day.

The author of Mark's Gospel remains a mystery because nowhere in the Gospel does the author identify himself. However, a tradition dating back to the early second century tells us he was a man named John Mark. If this is the same John Mark who appears in the Acts of the Apostles and in some of the epistles, we have more information on him than on many of the other Scripture writers. The Acts of the Apostles recounts that he and his cousin, Barnabas, helped St. Paul preach the Gospel to the Gentiles, but Paul got angry when John Mark abruptly left them during one of their missionary journeys. Acts 12:12 says that John Mark's mother's name was Mary and that some of the early Christians gathered at her house for prayer. Although they cannot prove it, some people believe this same house was both the site of the Last Supper and the location where the followers of Jesus waited for the coming of the Holy Spirit on Pentecost.

Many people assume that Mark was one of the apostles but that is not correct (his name does not appear on any of the lists of the Twelve in the New Testament). Not being an eyewitness to all the events he wrote about, Mark relied on others for his information.

Papias, one of the early church fathers, says that Mark was Peter's interpreter. If so, Mark was present when Peter preached about Jesus and sat at Peter's feet listening to him reminisce about the good old days when he and the other apostles traveled with the Lord throughout Palestine, preaching about the kingdom of God, debating with the scribes and the Pharisees, and healing those who were sick. Peter's memories are most likely one of the sources for Mark's Gospel.

For Reflection

Does it make a difference to you that Jesus experienced the same emotions you and I experience? If the Gospels did not tell us Jesus felt any emotions, would it be easier or more difficult to relate to him? Why or why not?

17th Sunday in Ordinary Time

John 6:1-15

Bread was one of the main foods in Jesus' day and it was part of every meal. Most people ate wheat bread but the poor made their bread from barley, a grain farmers often used as animal feed because it was so abundant. Thus, the boy with the barley bread in today's Gospel did not come from a well-to-do family.

Fish was the main source of protein in first-century Palestine because it was more plentiful and considerably cheaper than meat. Since there was no refrigeration in those days, fishermen either dried their catch in the sun or smoked it in shacks on the shore if they were to keep it for any length of time.

In today's Gospel, the apostles fill twelve baskets with the leftovers after everyone is done eating. You might be wondering where that many baskets came from. To answer this question, it is necessary to take a good look at Jewish dietary laws.

Jewish laws in Sacred Scripture spell out which foods the Jews may eat and forbids all others. Sea creatures that have fins and scales are edible and so are most fowl. However, the law says Jews can consume only land animals that both chew their cud and have a split hoof. (That's why Jews do not eat pork—pigs have a split hoof but they don't chew their cud.) The animals also must be properly slaughtered with a very sharp knife cutting the jugular vein so death is quick and painless. The Jews call foods that meet the above conditions *kosher*. Ancient Jews observed kosher dietary laws in biblical times and some pious Jews still follow them today in obedience to God's commands in Scripture and as a visible sign that being God's chosen ones makes them different from everyone else.

Dietary laws made it difficult for first-century Jews to travel to distant lands since there was no guarantee they would be able to get kosher food on the way. Therefore, many Jews, including Jesus and the apostles, carried large baskets of kosher food with them whenever they traveled anywhere. In today's Gospel, the apostles use their baskets to collect the leftover food.

For Reflection

Jesus gave thanks to his Father before passing out the food. Take time today to thank God for the food on your table and for those who prepared and served it. Pray for those who work in soup kitchens and for meals-on-wheels programs. Consider making a donation to a soup kitchen or an organization that feeds the poor.

18th Sunday in Ordinary Time

John 6:24-35

In today's Gospel, some people ask Jesus what they must do to perform the works of God. Jesus responds by saying they must have faith in the One whom God sent. "The One" was a title for the messiah, the military/political leader whom God would send to free the Jewish people from the oppression of their enemies.

From the reaction of the people, it appears they think Jesus' answer means he is claiming to be the messiah. Not wanting to let Jesus get away with making such a bold statement without backing it up, they challenge him to produce a sign proving he actually is who he says he is. This sign has a lot to do with the story about Moses in today's Old Testament reading.

In that reading (Exodus 16), the Jewish people complain to Moses that they have nothing to eat and God responds by sending them manna and quail. Later (Exodus 17), the people grumble because they have no water to drink so God tells Moses to strike a rock with his walking stick. Immediately, water flows from the rock.

Because the rabbis taught that the messiah would be even greater than Moses, some people expected the messiah to give them food and drink just as Moses did.

Therefore, when the people ask Jesus for a sign, they are challenging him to match Moses' feat by also giving them food from heaven.

Jesus accepts the challenge and says the food he gives is his body and the drink is his blood. Moses satisfied physical hunger and physical thirst but Jesus satisfies spiritual hunger and spiritual thirst. The Jews who ate the manna in the desert and drank the water from the rock were soon hungry and thirsty again, but Jesus will forever satisfy the spiritual hunger of those who eat his body and drink his blood. This indicates Jesus is greater than Moses and, therefore, the messiah.

For Reflection

Today's Gospel ends with Jesus saying he is the Bread of Life. Bread is symbolic of food and we need food to sustain life. What do you think Jesus meant when he claimed to be the Bread of Life?

19th Sunday in Ordinary Time

John 6:41-51

In recent Sunday Gospel readings from the Gospel according to John, Jesus tells us he is the bread of life come down from heaven and if we eat his body and drink his blood we will have eternal life. The bread of life is an important theme in John's Gospel because it refers to the bread and wine we share in the Eucharist.

Many people are surprised to learn that John's Gospel contains two stories of the Last Supper (see John 13:1-14:31 and 15:1-17:26). What's strange about the second story is that it doesn't add any new details. Because everything in it is also in the first story, biblical scholars aren't sure why the author included this second Last Supper story in the Gospel.

What's even stranger is that neither of John's Last Supper accounts say anything about Jesus blessing the bread and wine and sharing them with his disciples and neither of them tell us about the bread and wine being Jesus' body and blood. We find these very important details in each of the Last Supper stories of the other three Gospels but they are not part of John's narratives.

However, we should not conclude that John has nothing to say about what Jesus did with the bread and wine at the Last Supper. On the contrary, John's Gospel has more on this topic than any of the other three Gospels but his explanation is not part of his Last Supper accounts. Scripture scholars believe John explains the meaning of Jesus' actions in the sixth chapter immediately after the story about Jesus feeding the crowd with a few loaves and fishes, the same chapter from which recent Sunday Gospel readings have come from.

John gives so much space to this topic because gathering for the breaking of the bread was important to first-century Christians. The Eucharist was a vital part of their faith because it was both a sign of the continued presence of the risen Lord and a sign of their unity with each other. It would have been impossible for someone to claim to be a follower of Jesus and not take part in the Eucharistic celebrations.

For Reflection

How important is the Eucharist for you? Do you celebrate it each Sunday because you feel obligated or because you really want to? Pray that the Lord will help you to better appreciate the Eucharist.

20th Sunday in Ordinary Time

John 6:51-58

In today's Gospel, Jesus promises that whoever eats his flesh and drinks his blood will have eternal life. Most Christians believe that when Jesus spoke these words he was referring to the bread and wine we use in the celebration of the Lord's Supper.

We'll probably never know why Jesus chose bread instead of a lamb, a goat, or some other food or why he chose wine instead of milk, water, or some other liquid. What we do know is that bread and wine became powerful symbols of the Christian community.

Just as we grind many grains of wheat to make bread and press many grapes to make wine, many people come together to make up the Church. When we bring the bread and the wine to the altar, what we are offering is not just bread and wine but all those who have been baptized into God's family.

The bread and the wine also symbolize our own personal gifts to God. Anyone who baked bread in the days before food processors became popular knows that kneading dough calls for a lot of muscle. Therefore, bread is symbolic of hard work and when we bring our bread to God we offer him all the effort and all the sweat of our labors.

Wine is a symbol of joy because we often drink it at parties and on special occasions. When we bring our gift of wine to the altar, we offer God all the good times of our life and we invite him to become part of those good times.

For Reflection

Jesus is interested not only in our problems but also in our joys. The next time something good happens to you, bring that event to Jesus in prayer and tell him how you feel about it just as you would share that same news with a friend. Jesus really does care.

21st Sunday in Ordinary Time

John 6:60-69

The term "eternal life" appears not only in today's Gospel reading but also in the Gospel readings of the last couple of Sundays. In each of these readings, Jesus promises eternal life to anyone who eats his body and drinks his blood. Let's take a closer look at what this promise really means.

Although people sometimes use the terms "eternal life" and "immortality" interchangeably, the two terms really do not mean the same thing even though they both describe something that will never end. The distinction between these two terms becomes clear, however, when we focus on the beginning of what they describe rather than their ending. An immortal person or did not always exist; he or she had a beginning. On the other hand, an eternal person always existed; there was never a time when it didn't exist and there won't be a time when it won't exist. We have to understand this distinction when trying to grasp the meaning of Jesus' teaching in today's Gospel.

Notice that Jesus does not promise us immortality but eternal life. Since God is the only being who has always existed, only God possesses eternal life. Therefore, when Jesus promises eternal life to those who eat his body and drink his blood, he is promising that God will share his own life with them.

Normally, we share our lives only with the people whom we love and those whom we consider special. Therefore, we can conclude that God offers to share his life with us because he loves us and because he considers us special. This is a central teaching of our Christian faith as well as one of its greatest mysteries.

For Reflection

Relationships don't just happen. We need to work on them and develop them. What specific steps are you taking to strengthen your relationship with God? How much time and effort do you devote each day to developing this relationship?

22nd Sunday in Ordinary Time

Mark 7:1-8, 14-15, 21-23

The oral traditions were interpretations of the laws God gave to Moses on Mt. Sinai which explained how the Jews were to apply the laws in everyday life. At first, the rabbis did not write down these interpretations but passed them on by word of mouth.

By Jesus' time, some of the scribes who belonged to one group of Pharisees considered the oral traditions as important as the laws themselves, so they taught that a person who wanted to be holy had to follow both the 613 oral traditions and the laws in Sacred Scripture. All people who failed to observe them, even those who didn't know what they were and those who accidentally broke one, were sinners.

Some oral traditions outlined how Jews were to wash their hands before eating a meal and spelled out in detail such things as which direction they should point their fingers when they poured water over them, how much water they should use, and the type of container they should store the water in. Overlooking nothing, the oral traditions even gave an exact step-by-step procedure describing how one hand should wash the other!

Anyone who did not observe these oral traditions was ritually unclean. This did not mean the person was dirty, but it did prevent the person from taking part in any formal religious worship. An unclean person had to go through even more rituals to be cleansed of the impurity.

One could also become unclean by coming in contact with something touched by an unclean person. Therefore, pious Jews often sprinkled food they purchased in the marketplace with water because they did not know who touched it. Likewise, they washed plates, cups, jugs, and utensils in a special way before using them.

In today's Gospel, Jesus objects to these oral traditions because they became more important than how one treated family and friends. Jesus points out that being hateful, or gossipy, or adulterous is much more serious than failing to properly wash hands or utensils before eating. We do not find holiness in a ritual but in how we treat one another.

For Reflection

We cannot go to church each Sunday (perform the proper ritual) and hate our neighbor the rest of the week. Take time today to examine how you treat others. Is there anyone whom you treat poorly? Make an effort this week to get along better with this person.

23rd Sunday in Ordinary Time

Mark 7:31-37

The story in today's Gospel begins with some people bringing to Jesus a deaf man who had a speech impediment. Taking him aside, Jesus puts his fingers into the man's ears and touches the man's tongue with spittle. Looking upward as if he is asking his heavenly Father for assistance, Jesus says to the man "*Ephphatha*," an Aramaic word that means "be open." Immediately, the man is able to hear and he begins to speak clearly.

While it may sound a little crude to us, touching the man's tongue with saliva was an accepted medical practice. After observing animals licking their wounds to ward off infections, ancient people concluded that if saliva could promote healing in an animal it would also help human beings. However, because the people in Jesus' day did not understand how or why saliva worked, they thought they could use it to cure all kinds of ailments, including blindness, deafness, and speech problems.

Since Greek is the original language of the Gospels, some people wonder why the evangelist did not translate an Aramaic word like "ephphatha" into its Greek equivalent. Because Aramaic was the everyday language of first-century Palestinian Jews, including Jesus and the apostles, biblical scholars think the Gospel writer preserved "Ephphatha" (and a few other Aramaic words we find in the Gospels) in its original language because Jesus actually spoke this word on the occasion described in the story. The written accounts of what Jesus said, although accurately reflecting the substance of his message, are not word-for-word transcripts of his sermons.

The fact that Mark tells us what "ephphatha" means indicates his audience did not know Aramaic and was probably not Jewish. Therefore, Mark most likely wrote his Gospel for Gentile Christians.

For Reflection

Thank God for giving you the ability hear and to speak. Pray this week for those who are unable to do so. Pray also for those who work with the hearing impaired and for speech therapists.

24th Sunday in Ordinary Time

Mark 8:27-35

In today's Gospel, Jesus says we have to deny ourselves and take up our cross if we want to follow him. He promises whoever saves his life will lose it and whoever gives his life for him and for the Gospel will save it. Although taking up one's cross can mean accepting life's pains and disappointments, there is another possible interpretation.

In ancient times, very religious Jews who wanted to give their lives completely to God symbolically traced the Hebrew letter *tau* on their forehead. A tau looks like a + or an X. When a person traced it on the forehead, it meant the person belonged to God, similar to the brand put on cattle to identify their owner.

Since the tau resembled a cross, someone who dedicated their life to God in this way took up the cross. Therefore, the expression "to take up one's cross" can mean giving one's life to God. When Jesus says we have to deny ourselves and take up our cross to follow him, he is talking about dedicating ourselves to him. Those who save their lives (keep their lives for themselves) are the people who do not give their lives over to him. These people are more concerned with their own pleasures than with pleasing God and, because of this, they will lose their chance at eternal life with Jesus in heaven.

On the other hand, those who give their lives for Jesus' sake (freely dedicate themselves to him) live for God rather than for self. God will reward them with eternal life.

Instead of tracing the tau on their foreheads, the early Christians dedicated themselves to Jesus by placing their right hand on their left shoulder and their left hand on their right shoulder, thus making an X (*tau*) across their chest. This practice gradually evolved into what Catholics and some other Christians now call "making the sign of the cross." The sign of the cross is like our brand mark with which we identify ourselves as belonging to the Father, and to the Son, and to the Holy Spirit.

For Reflection

Are you ready to lose your life for Jesus (give yourself to him) or are you holding something back (saving your life for yourself)? Pray that you will be able to give more of yourself to Jesus.

25th Sunday in Ordinary Time

Mark 9:30-37

The Old Testament, in some instances, uses the term "Son of Man" as a title for the messiah (savior). We find one such example in the book of Daniel, where the author writes about four powerful but cruel rulers who attempt to conquer the world. In the Jewish mind, these rulers are so ruthless that the author pictures them as four fear-inspiring and hideous beasts (e.g., a leopard with four heads, a beast with ten horns, etc.). After the fourth beast rules, God sends the son of man to conquer the world and then rule not like an animal that instills fear but rather like a human being, with justice and compassion.

The apostles also have this picture of a messiah who will be victorious. Therefore, they do not understand what Jesus means when he tells them in today's Gospel that the son of man will be handed over to his enemies and be put to death. That simply was not supposed to happen.

Believing Jesus is the messiah, the apostles think of themselves as generals in his army who will share in his victories and be highly respected by the Jewish people. Feeling important, they begin to argue about which one of them ranks the highest. Overhearing their discussion, Jesus tells them that if they want to be great, they have to become lowly servants and must even welcome children for his sake.

Palestine was a dry and dusty land where people wore sandals on their feet. The master of the house usually welcomed his guests by washing their feet himself or by instructing a servant to do it. The more insignificant the guest, the more humiliating this task was. Washing the feet of a rabbi or a prominent politician was not as degrading as washing the feet of a fisherman or a shepherd. Since children were on the bottom rung of the social ladder, welcoming a child (washing the child's feet) was the lowliest of jobs, a very humbling task. This is the type of humility, a humility that compels a person to serve the poorest of the poor and the least significant of society, that should distinguish Jesus' followers.

For Reflection

Pray for the ability to be more humble. Do something special this week for someone who would least expect your help.

26th Sunday in Ordinary Time

Mark 9:38-43, 45, 47-48

At one time, kings tried to marry the daughter of the king of a stronger nation because the stronger king would not likely declare war on a land where his daughter lived. However, kings who married foreign women often ended up worshiping their wife's gods. In pagan countries, this did not cause a problem since pagans not only believed there were many gods but also often worshiped several gods at the same time. The Jews, on the other hand, believed there was only one true God. Therefore, Jewish kings who married foreign wives were exposing themselves to a dangerous influence that might lead them to be unfaithful to their Jewish beliefs. For this reason, the Old Testament prophets often warned the Jewish kings not to marry foreign women.

The Bible tells us that some of the Jewish kings did indeed take foreign wives and, as the prophets predicted, they began worshiping pagan gods. Because the pagans believed a few of these gods demanded human sacrifice, some Jewish kings sacrificed their own children to the gods in an attempt to appease them.

In today's Gospel reading, Jesus says that it would be better to cut off a hand and enter eternal life maimed than to end up in Gehenna with both hands intact. The

Hebrew word *Gehenna* means "valley of Hinnom" which was a ravine located southwest of the city of Jerusalem where some Old Testament Jewish kings offered their children as holocaust sacrifices to the pagan god Molech. Its history led the Jews to believe the valley of Hinnom was good for nothing except for dumping garbage. Because the smell from the trash accumulating there was terrible and smoke from smoldering fires always covered the area, Gehenna was good only as a breeding place for worms thriving on the garbage.

Gehenna was so repulsive that some Jews who believed in a life after death used it as a symbol of the punishment awaiting all those who led wicked lives. Worms ate those who were in Gehenna and flames continuously consumed them. According to some of the rabbis, the only relief came on the Sabbath, when God had mercy and caused the fires to cease. Biblical scholars sometimes translate Gehenna as "hell," even though the two concepts differ in significant ways.

For Reflection

God lets us choose if we want to be with him or not. We don't make our choice known verbally but rather by how we live our lives. Based on your lifestyle, is there any doubt about what your choice is?

27th Sunday in Ordinary Time

Mark 10:2-16

The Jewish faith has a great respect for marriage, but it also recognizes that divorce is possible under certain conditions. In Deuteronomy 24:1, there is a law permitting a man to divorce his wife if he finds some "indecency" in her. In Jesus' day, there were two different ways the rabbis interpreted this passage.

One group of rabbis taught indecency meant adultery and they believed a man could divorce his wife only if she was unfaithful to him. Another group said indecency pertained to trivial matters like being a lousy cook or embarrassing her husband in public. You can guess which of these two interpretations of the law was more popular.

Although the man could divorce his wife, the wife could not divorce her husband without his permission. Even then, Jewish law recognized only a few conditions under which this was possible (e.g., if he became a leper or raped a virgin). This unequal treatment undoubtedly was the result of the male dominated society.

When a man decided to divorce his wife, he had only to write a note declaring his intention to divorce her (that's the decree of divorce in today's Gospel) and then give this note to her in the presence of witnesses. It was that easy!

Quoting Genesis 2, Jesus rejects the liberal understanding of divorce and says marriage is forever. A man who divorces his wife and marries another commits adultery. Likewise, a woman who divorces her husband and marries another man also commits adultery.

This teaching poses many problems for Christians who want to uphold the sanctity of marriage but also want to show compassion for those who realize they made a mistake. Did Jesus mean that a couple who are in a bad marriage must either stay married for the rest of their lives or remain single if they choose to get a divorce? Or was Jesus speaking about the ideal for which all of us should strive but not necessarily attain?

Different Christian denominations answer these questions in a variety of ways, some permitting divorce and remarriage, others prohibiting it, and still others granting annulments. The one thing certain about this issue is that it will continue to be the focus of theological and scriptural debates for many years to come.

For Reflection

Because divorce is often a very painful experience, those who are going through it need to be supported and prayed for, not condemned. Pray today for someone you know who is going through divorce proceedings. If possible, call or write to let this person know you still care.

28th Sunday in Ordinary Time

Mark 10:17-30

When Jesus says in today's Gospel that it is difficult for a rich man to enter the kingdom of God, the apostles can't believe their ears because, like many of the other Jews of their day, they thought the rich had the best shot at being holy.

The Jews considered their laws to be a road map to holiness. A person who followed the laws was holy and someone who broke a law (even if they didn't know what it was) was a sinner. Since most poor people had to work long hours for the basic necessities of life, they didn't have the time to study and learn all the Jewish laws in Scripture and tradition. Therefore, holiness was out of their reach.

Because the rich didn't have to work so hard, they were able to devote more of their time to learning the interpretations of the law and had a better chance at being holy. Some of them even believed their prosperity was a sign that God was indeed pleased with them.

When Jesus says it is easier for a camel to pass through the eye of a needle than for a rich man to enter the kingdom of God, he isn't talking about a sewing needle. Instead, he may be referring to a gate of the city of Jerusalem.

Ancient people built high walls around their cities for protection from hostile armies. They opened gates in the walls in the morning and closed these gates at dusk so invaders could not enter the city at night and capture it while everyone slept. The city of Jerusalem had seven main gates and several smaller ones. These gates were narrow and low so the enemy could not ride in on horseback but would first have to dismount and then proceed in on foot. The people of Jerusalem nicknamed one low and narrow gate "the eye of the needle."

Although this gate kept the enemy out, it also made it difficult for traders who came from distant lands (often with camels laden with heavy, bulky packages) to get into the city. The trader had to unload all the goods from the camel, get the camel to bend down and squeeze through the gate, carry the goods through the gate himself, and then reload the camel. This whole process was time-consuming, hard work.

Jesus is saying in today's Gospel that just as it is difficult for a camel to get through the eye of the needle because of the baggage, it is difficult for the rich to enter the kingdom of God. "If it's hard for a rich man to be holy," the apostles must have reasoned, "then what chance do poor fishermen like us have?" Jesus tells them not to despair because he doesn't measure holiness by what a person owns, but by what one is willing to give up in order to follow him. Whoever sacrifices family and possessions for the sake of the Gospel will have everlasting life.

For Reflection

Would you be willing to sacrifice some of your own wealth to spread the Gospel? Be honest!

29th Sunday in Ordinary Time

Mark 10:35-45

In today's Gospel, James and John ask Jesus if they could sit at his right and at his left when he comes into his glory. Like many of the Jews of that day, these two brothers were expecting a political/military messiah through whom God would defeat their enemies, conquer the world, and establish a kingdom of justice and peace (that's what they meant when they talked about Jesus coming into his glory).

The seats on either side of the royal throne were places of honor the king reserved for the prime minister and the prince successor. Those who sat in these seats were in a very powerful position because, unlike everyone else who had to request a special audience with the king and perhaps wait days or weeks for the opportunity to talk to him, they merely had to lean over and whisper in the king's ear. Therefore, we can conclude that James' and John's request to sit at Jesus' right and left was nothing less than a bold attempt to gain power by trying to get Jesus to guarantee they would occupy the places of honor when he, the messiah, established his kingdom. There are two explanations why James and John thought they deserved special treatment.

Scripture scholars believe James and John were probably part of Jesus' inner circle of disciples because whenever the Gospels list the twelve apostles, they always name Peter first and James and John second and third. It seems like Jesus favored these three apostles and even allowed them to witness events the other apostles did not (e.g., the transfiguration and when Jesus brought a little girl back to life).

According to three of the Gospels (Matthew, Mark, and Luke), James and John were fishing with their father Zebedee and the hired hands when Jesus called them to be his disciples. Zebedee's fishing business must have been providing him with a comfortable living if he was able to employ not only his own sons, but others as well. Therefore, since James and John were from a more financially prosperous family than most people, including the other apostles, they may have thought they were better and deserved special honors.

Tradition tells us all of the apostles were martyrs except John. However, today's Gospel ends with Jesus predicting that John, too, will die for his faith. Was John a martyr or did he live to a ripe old age? No one knows for sure.

For Reflection

The apostles experienced petty jealousies and they competed for Jesus' attention and approval. Jesus told them not to worry about who was the greatest but to focus on serving others. Make a list of the people you can or do serve.

30th Sunday in Ordinary Time

Mark 10:46-52

In today's Gospel, a blind beggar calls Jesus the Son of David. Since Jesus' father was Joseph, who is this other person the blind man is talking about?

David who, according to the Bible, was both a shepherd boy and a skilled harpist, was a very important figure in the history of the Jewish people. He was the same David who used a slingshot to kill Goliath, the Philistine giant, and he later became the greatest king of the Jews.

As king, David first made Jerusalem the capital of the Jewish nation; then ordered the Ark of the Covenant (the chest in which the Jews kept the Ten Commandments) be brought there. At that time, the Jews housed the Ark (a visible sign of God's presence) in a special tent.

One of the first things David did after becoming king was build himself a palace of the finest materials but it wasn't long before he began feeling a little guilty about living in luxury while the Ark of the Covenant was in a tent. Therefore, David decided he would build a house for the Lord, a magnificent temple unequaled by any other building in the world. However, in a dream God told the prophet Nathan that David should not carry out his plans. Instead, God would build a house (a dynasty) for David and would bless it with peace and prosperity. Furthermore, God said one of David's descendants would occupy the throne forever.

At first, the Jews understood God's promises to mean David's son would rule after him and his son's son would rule after that and so on. Historically, that did not prove to be true because one military power after another conquered the Jewish nation and executed the last of the Jewish kings.

Since God would not lie, the Jews reasoned they must have misunderstood what he meant and concluded that God's promises referred to a future descendant of David. They believed this descendant or Son of David would be the messiah who would conquer the world and rule forever with peace and justice.

So, when Bartimaeus calls Jesus "Son of David" instead of "Son of Joseph," he acknowledges that Jesus is the promised messiah, the descendant of David through whom God would fulfill his promises.

For Reflection

Being unable to see is only one type of blindness. We can also be spiritually blind when we fail to see how God is working in our lives. Pray this week that you will recognize the many ways the Lord shows his love for you everyday.

31st Sunday in Ordinary Time

Mark 12:28-34

Jewish men had more education than most people in the ancient world even though they knew only enough to be able to read from the Scriptures when the leader of the synagogue called upon them to do so during synagogue services. By today's standards, most people of the first century A.D. were illiterate.

A scribe was an important person because he was one of the few people who could read and write fluently. People relied on scribes to copy laws onto parchment scrolls and to draw up contracts and treaties. Some Jewish scribes spent their time copying the Jewish Scriptures, a very tedious task because the rabbis decreed a scroll could not be used in synagogue services if it contained more than two copying mistakes. Because they didn't have erasers, the scribes had to be very careful.

The Jewish people call their Scriptures the Torah, a word that literally means "the law" because it contains the laws God gave to Moses on Mt. Sinai. The Torah includes the books of Genesis, Exodus, Leviticus, Numbers, and Deuteronomy—the same five books we find at the beginning of the Christian Bible.

The Jews expected the scribes who copied the books of the Torah not only to know all of the Jewish laws but also to interpret them. The scribes debated among themselves about such things as whether or not the law permitted someone to eat an egg laid by a chicken on the Sabbath and how far one could walk on the Sabbath before breaking the commandment to keep holy the Lord's day.

Soon, the scribes created 613 new laws (called the oral traditions) to clarify the original laws God gave to Moses. The scribes then challenged each other to sum up all of these laws at once in as few words as possible. The scribe in today's Gospel is asking Jesus to do just that.

Jesus responds with Deuteronomy 6:4, a passage which says there is only one God and we should love him with all our heart, soul, mind, and strength. The Jewish people call this passage the *shema* (Hebrew for "hear," the first word of this verse), and they regard it as a fundamental teaching of their faith.

The second part of Jesus' answer is that we should love our neighbor as ourselves and is from Leviticus 19:18. Linking these two passages is what makes Jesus' response unique because by doing so Jesus proclaims that we cannot love God unless we also love our neighbor.

For Reflection

Jesus challenges his followers to be great lovers. Love is more than a feeling; it is wanting what is best for someone and being willing to do whatever we can for that person. Is it possible, then, to love someone you don't like?

32nd Sunday in Ordinary Time

Mark 12:38-44

Because the scribes were able to read and write, most people in the first century respected them for their intelligence. Some of these learned scholars loved all the attention they got and did everything they could to get even more of the spotlight.

In today's Gospel, Jesus criticizes the scribes of the Pharisee party for wearing long robes and accepting marks of respect in public. The robes may have been the wide, scarf-like prayer shawl (called the Tallit) that Jews wore only while praying. Some scribes continued wearing these prayer shawls long after they finished reciting their prayers so others would see they had been praying and would think they were holy.

These scribes also preferred sitting in the synagogue's front seats which the town's dignitaries usually occupied. Many of them coveted the seat in the very front because it faced the congregation and everyone present noticed those who sat there. The seats farthest back were for the lower classes, women, and children.

Jesus criticizes these scribes because they did not perform their actions out of genuine holiness but because they wanted the attention of others. Their intentions were very different from that of the poor widow in today's Gospel.

In the Temple, there were thirteen trumpet-shaped chests for collecting offerings, each for a specific purpose (e.g., to buy oil for the lamps in the Temple). Rich people probably got everyone's attention by going from chest to chest putting in their offerings as everyone watched them. Since ancient people did not use paper money, the sound of the coins hitting the inside of the metallic trumpet made it obvious how much money they gave. While his apostles observe this happening, Jesus calls their attention to the poor widow who quietly contributes only a few small coins. This woman's holiness exceeded that of the scribes and the rich because she didn't give to be noticed by others but to be noticed by God.

For Reflection

All of us are sometimes like the scribes. We want to be noticed and we want others to think well of us. How much are you motivated by what others will say or think about you?

33rd Sunday in Ordinary Time

Mark 13:24-32

Today's Gospel is an example of apocalyptic writing, a special type of literature that uses symbolic language and deals with both a specific historical situation as well as the end of time. For instance, some biblical scholars believe the words in today's Gospel describe what happened when the Romans captured Jerusalem in 70 A.D. but many people also think this reading refers to the end of the world.

Because enemies were usually persecuting the intended audience, the authors of apocalyptic writings used symbolic language to give hope without risking increased persecution should the writing fall into the wrong hands. For instance, if the author simply tried to encourage his people to persevere by saying the king will one day die and his oppressive tactics will end, there was the possibility the king may intercept this writing and persecute his subjects even more because of it. However, if the author writes that the lion (the king) with the ten horns (symbolizing power) will one day be slain, the king will not know what this means and will probably dismiss it as gibberish.

The author of the words in today's Gospel reading addresses early Christians whom the Romans were persecuting and killing because of their faith in the risen Lord. Mark tells them that even though they have to endure many terrifying ordeals (the reference to the sun and the moon being darkened is symbolic apocalyptic language for trials and tribulations) they should remain faithful to Jesus who promises to save them. Mark quotes Jesus as saying that even if heaven and earth pass away, he will still fulfill his promise to be with them in their time of need.

We have to remember that authors of apocalyptic literature wrote to give hope, not to instill fear. The message of apocalyptic writings is that no matter how bad the situation becomes, God will intervene in history and will vindicate those who remain faithful to him. Therefore, anyone who uses apocalyptic writings like the book of Revelation to scare us is either deliberately misusing Scripture or really does not understand it.

For Reflection

According to New Testament apocalyptic writings, those of us who believe in Jesus have nothing to fear because he is more powerful than anything else. All we need to do is put our faith and trust in him and he'll take care of the rest. Do you trust the Lord enough to do that or do you tend to rely on your own power and abilities?

Trinity Sunday

Matthew 28:16-20

Since Jesus was Jewish, we shouldn't be surprised that most of his active ministry took place in Jewish cities. Rarely do we find him preaching or healing in non-Jewish (Gentile) territory. From the Acts of the Apostles, we learn that the early Christians, like Jesus, also preached mainly to the Jews.

Being God's chosen people, many Jews believed they were God's instrument in the world and that God planned to work through them in a special way. Basing their conclusions on Scripture, some rabbis taught that God intended to send the Jewish people a messiah who would conquer and rule the world through them.

The Jews were understandably proud of their status as God's favorite nation but their pride sometimes led to snobbishness. Many Jews did not want anything to do with Gentiles and even believed contact with Gentiles made them ritually impure. Therefore, pious Jews didn't talk to Gentiles and didn't associate with them in any way. After passing through Gentile territory, some Jews even shook the dirt from their sandals before stepping onto Jewish soil because they did not want the Promised Land contaminated by Gentile dust.

Since most early Christians were Jews who shared these attitudes (no, they weren't perfect), they initially limited their preaching to the Jewish people. Only later did the early Christians understand Jesus' command to make disciples of *all* nations and begin preaching to all people, not just to the Jews.

We don't have much biblical evidence about what most of the apostles did or where they went after they received the gift of the Holy Spirit on Pentecost, but tradition tells us they took Jesus' words seriously and traveled to distant lands to preach the Gospel. According to tradition, Nathaniel and Thomas went to India, James to Spain, and other apostles to France, Great Britain, Mesopotamia, Ethiopia, and even to what is now Russia. Those who heard them and believed were baptized "in the name of the Father, and of the Son, and of the Holy Spirit."

For Reflection

Pray today for missionaries who preach the Gospel in distant lands. Pray that they may have the wisdom needed to clearly explain the Good News about Jesus and that they will have the courage to proclaim God's love even when others persecute them for doing so.

Corpus Christi

Mark 14:12-16, 22-26

When people in biblical times entered into an agreement, they didn't draw up a contract and sign it because most of them did not know how to read or write. Instead, they sealed the agreement by going through a little ceremony. That's exactly what happens in today's first reading.

In that reading, Moses stands at the foot of the mountain and, after reading the conditions of the agreement, he takes the blood of young bulls and sprinkles some of it on the altar and the rest on the people. As he does this, he says the blood is that of the covenant God is making with the Jewish people. In this way, Moses and the people ratify the covenant or contract that they enter into with the Lord. In this contract, they promise to obey the commandments and the Lord promises he will take care of them because they are his special people.

Although the ceremonies used to ratify an agreement differed from time to time and from place to place, there was one thing they had in common. Blood was always an important part of these ceremonies because ancient people believed blood was the source of life. They used the blood of animals as a symbolic way of saying that the agreement was coming to life. The shedding of blood made the agreement official.

In today's Gospel reading, Jesus takes the cup of wine and says it is his blood, the blood of the covenant. Jesus used his own blood to give life to a new covenant between his followers and his Father in heaven. Jesus' blood made our covenant with God official.

Notice that all three of today's readings contain the word "covenant." The dictionary defines this word as "a contract or agreement." Although this isn't an incorrect definition, it really isn't an adequate one either.

A covenant is a contract or agreement in which the parties who are entering into the agreement share their lives with each other. A covenant involves a relationship, a very close relationship built on love. It was Jesus' blood that made such a close and loving relationship between God and us a reality.

For Reflection

God wants to share his life with us but he will not force himself into our lives. Take time today to invite God into your life. Ask him to teach you how to love as he loves.

Christt the King

John 18:33-37

Sometimes historical and political situations have influenced the ways Christians picture Jesus. Thus, when monarchs ruled nations and empires, the popular image people had of Jesus was that of the King of Kings, an image that reminded them that Jesus ruled the universe.

This emphasis on Jesus as a divine ruler eventually led the Church to designate the last Sunday of the liturgical year (that's today) as the Feast of Christ the King. Like the other images of Jesus, this image also has biblical support.

In today's Gospel, Pilate asks Jesus if he is a king and Jesus' response is that he is indeed a ruler but his kingdom is not of this world. Elsewhere in the Bible, Jesus tells a parable in which he refers to himself as a king who separates the good from the bad (Matthew 25:31-46) and, when he rides into the city of Jerusalem on a donkey (Luke 19:28-40), the people treat him as if he is royalty. These are only a few examples of passages that speak of Jesus' kingship.

In biblical times, as today, it was a great honor to be in the presence of the king because he did not give everyone this privilege, and he granted even fewer individuals an audience with him. As the king entered the room, all present bowed their heads and fell to their knees, acknowledging him as their lord and master. Without a sound from anyone, the king then ascended his throne and began to discharge his royal duties.

Because Jesus has become so familiar to us, we sometimes forget that he is our king and we don't always appreciate how privileged we are to be guaranteed an audience with our king whenever we want one. Unlike earthly kings, we can confidently bring our needs before Jesus' heavenly throne, knowing he will listen to us and will not turn us away. No earthly king would ever be so accessible to his subjects.

For Reflection

Kings are sometimes addressed as "my lord." What does the word "lord" mean? What do we mean when we call Jesus "our Lord and master"? Is Jesus really Lord of your life?

Cycle C

1st Sunday of Advent

Luke 21:25-28, 34-36

Unlike the calendar year, which begins on January 1, the Church's liturgical year begins on the first Sunday of Advent. Each new Church year uses a different set of Sunday Scripture readings.

Most of the Gospel readings for the Sundays of the next twelve months will be from the Gospel according to Luke. So let's begin this liturgical year by examining what we know about the author of this Gospel.

Scripture scholars are certain the author of Luke's Gospel also wrote the Acts of the Apostles, a book about the early Church. However, nowhere in either of these writings does the author tell us his name. Irenaeus, a bishop living at the end of the second century, was the first to identify the author as Luke, a companion of St. Paul.

Epistles attributed to Paul mention Luke three times and one of these passages calls him a physician, meaning he probably made salves and other medicines out of herbs and roots. Luke was not an apostle and, therefore, was not an eyewitness to the events he records.

Scripture scholars believe Luke probably wrote his Gospel around 85 A.D. and, like the Acts of the

Apostles, he addressed it to a man called Theophilus, a name meaning "friend of God." Some biblical scholars suggest Theophilus may have been a wealthy nobleman who provided the papyrus scroll (quite expensive in those days) on which Luke wrote the Gospel but other scholars hypothesize he was not a real person at all but was a character Luke created as a symbol of all Christians who were friends of God.

Today's Gospel begins with Jesus talking about the end of the world (another example of the same apocalyptic writing style we found in the Gospel reading a couple weeks ago) and it warns us to remain watchful and pray constantly because the great day when Jesus will return will suddenly close in on us. We should not be caught unprepared.

Most of us usually associate Advent with getting ready for the arrival of the baby Jesus but that's not what this liturgical season is all about. The soft and cuddly baby born in a manger has already come and gone. Today's Gospel tells us to prepare for Jesus' second coming, his arrival as the triumphant ruler of the universe. Therefore, during Advent, Christians should anxiously prepare for the return of the adult Jesus.

For Reflection

Don't let Advent pass by without taking some concrete steps to improve your relationship with the Lord. Pick a quiet time each day during which you will spend an extra ten or fifteen minutes in prayer. Do this faithfully and notice how it improves your relationship with God.

2nd Sunday of Advent

Luke 3:1-6

The strange names in today's Gospel are confusing, but they are very important because they help us identify the historical period during which Jesus lived and preached. Therefore, these names require a closer examination.

The reading begins with Luke telling us that Herod, Philip, and Lysanias were tetrarchs at the time when John the Baptist began preaching and that Pilate was procurator of Judea. "Tetrarch" is a Greek word that means "a ruler of one-fourth"; it refers to one of the four sections into which the Romans divided their provinces. "Procurator" is another word the Romans used for "governor."

When Herod the Great (the king of the Jews when Jesus was born) died in 4 B.C., the Romans divided his kingdom among three of his sons: Antipas, Archelaus, and Philip. Herod Antipas, the Herod Luke refers to in today's Gospel, ruled Galilee (where Jesus lived and spent most of his time preaching) until 39 A.D. Herod Philip ruled his part of the kingdom until 33 A.D. and Herod Archelaus reigned in his own territory until the Romans removed him from power in 25 A.D. and replaced him with a Roman governor named Pontius Pilate. Since Luke tells us Philip was still ruling and

Pilate was already in power when John's ministry began, the events in today's Gospel must have taken place between 25 and 33 A.D.

Luke helps narrow the date even further when he says John the Baptist began preaching during the fifteenth year of the reign of Tiberius. Since we know Tiberius Caesar became the sole emperor of Rome in 14 A.D., John's ministry had to begin about 28-29 A.D., with Jesus' own ministry beginning shortly thereafter.

Today's Gospel ends with Luke shifting his focus to John the Baptist, quoting John as telling the people to clear the way for the Lord. Kings in those days sent their messengers ahead of them before they visited a city or town. The messengers were responsible for helping the people prepare for the coming of the king. That's John's message to us today. He reminds us to get our hearts ready because our king, Jesus Christ, is on his way.

For Reflection

You spend time preparing for important events in your life (job interviews, parties, dates, etc.). How much time do you spend getting ready for Jesus? Isn't he more important?

3rd Sunday of Advent

Luke 3:10-18

Scripture scholars sometimes call Luke's Gospel the Gospel of the Holy Spirit because Luke, more than the other three evangelists, tries to make us aware of the action and the power of God's Spirit in the world. The term Holy Spirit appears thirteen times in Luke, five times in Matthew, four times in Mark, and only three times in John (although John uses other titles for the third person of the Blessed Trinity).

In today's reading, John the Baptist tells the people the messiah will baptize them in the Holy Spirit and in fire. Because fire is one of the most common symbols of God's presence, many of the religions of the world use fire or a light of some kind to symbolize that God is in their midst.

The reading ends with John the Baptist saying the messiah will clear the threshing floor with a winnowing fan and then gather the wheat into his barns. When a farmer harvested wheat in biblical times, he separated grain from the hulls by heaping the sheaves onto a threshing floor (a hard, flat, elevated area in an open field) and then pulverizing and crushing them with an ox or donkey pulling a heavy board with sharp stones attached. As the board passed over the wheat, the hulls (also known as chaff) cracked and the kernels that were inside fell out. The farmer then used a winnowing fan (also known as a winnowing fork because it looked like a large fork with tines that were very close together) to toss the chaff and the kernels into the air. The wind then blew away the light chaff but the heavy kernels fell to the ground. The farmer gathered these kernels into barns and later ground them into flour.

Winnowing was a symbol for divine judgment; the useless chaff the wind blew away represented wicked people, and the kernels the farmer gathered into the barns were those people who remained faithful to God. Therefore, in today's Gospel John tells his followers to prepare for the day of judgment by repenting of their sins and reforming their lives so they will be worthy to stand in the presence of their God.

For Reflection

By now you have probably spent a great deal of time preparing for the holidays. Take about fifteen minutes today (and every day until Christmas) to prepare your soul for the coming of your messiah, Jesus Christ.

4th Sunday of Advent

Luke 1:39-45

Today's Gospel begins after an angel informs Mary that she will be the mother of the messiah. Upon hearing the news that her relative, Elizabeth, is also expecting, Mary hurries off to visit her. The Gospels say Mary and Elizabeth were kinswomen, a term ancient Jews used to describe a variety of different relationships. Although popular tradition calls the two women cousins, there is nothing in Scripture to support this belief. However, because there is nothing to refute it either, we will never know the exact relationship between these two women.

In her greeting, Elizabeth says that both Mary and the fruit of her womb are blessed. The term "fruit of the womb" has an interesting history.

Because ancient people did not have the benefit of all the sophisticated medical equipment we have today, their understanding of the human reproductive system was rather primitive. They believed life was in the man's sperm which, they reasoned, was like a seed. Just as the seed contained life within itself and just as this life emerged once someone planted the seed in the ground, the man had to plant the sperm in the woman's womb. Therefore, they thought of the womb as the garden in which the seed would take root and grow.

With all of this agricultural symbolism, the next logical step was for them to begin calling the baby "the fruit of the womb." Thus, Jesus was the fruit of Mary's womb.

Last week, we learned that biblical scholars sometimes call Luke's Gospel the Gospel of the Holy Spirit because it talks so much about how the Spirit is working in the world. At times, they also call it the Gospel of Great Joy because the word "joy" appears so frequently (nine times). We find one of those occurrences in today's Gospel reading in which Luke quotes Elizabeth as saying the baby in her womb was moved with joy at the sound of Mary's greeting. Clearly, Luke considered the birth of the messiah a happy event.

For Reflection

Mary went to see Elizabeth to share the news of how God was working through her. How is God using you? Share that news with someone this week.

Please refer to Cycle A for the following commentaries:

Feast of the Holy Family

Luke 2:41-52

The Gospel according to Luke is the only Gospel that says anything about the years between Jesus' birth and the beginning of his public ministry. Today's reading is about the journey Joseph, Mary, and Jesus made to Jerusalem to celebrate the feast of Passover when Jesus was only twelve years old. Jewish law mandated all adult males living within fifteen miles of Jerusalem visit the Temple on three major feasts: Passover, Pentecost, and Tabernacles. Custom, however, required those living too far from the holy city to make the pilgrimage only during Passover.

The fact Jesus was twelve years old is significant because a Jewish boy became an adult at age thirteen, a milestone marked today by celebrating a bar-mitzvah. "Bar-mitzvah" means "son of the law"; it is a momentous event because from then on the boy must observe all Jewish laws, something the rabbis in Jesus' day considered women and children too weak to do.

Adulthood also brought the boy special honors. Prayers in the synagogue could not begin unless there were at least ten adult males present and only an adult male could read from the Torah scroll during the services. Therefore, to prepare for this privilege, Jewish boys usually attended the synagogue school where the rabbi taught them how to read from Sacred Scripture, making them more learned than other people in the world at that time.

Joseph and Mary probably took Jesus with them to Jerusalem to acquaint him with the Temple and its surroundings as part of his preparation for adulthood. Entire towns often made these pilgrimages to the Temple together, the women traveling as one group and the men as another group not far behind them. On their way home, Mary thought Jesus was with Joseph, and Joseph thought he was with Mary. The fact that several of Jesus' aunts, uncles, and cousins also lived in the same town and were probably traveling with the group also complicated things since this made it possible Jesus was with one of them.

Returning to Jerusalem, Joseph and Mary found Jesus in the Temple, listening to the rabbis and asking them questions, the Jewish way of describing a student learning from his teachers. Relieved but also a little angry, Mary scolded Jesus for making them look three days for him. Bewildered, Jesus responded to his mother with a comment that meant, "But Mom, I did what I thought was right. You know how eager I am to become an adult in our religion, so I stayed here in the Temple thinking that would be the first place you'd look for me." What mother could argue with that kind of logic?

For Reflection

Raising a child is not easy, even if the child is the Son of God. Pray today for all parents, especially those who are having difficulty with their children.

Baptism of the Lord

Luke 3:15-16, 21-22

The messiah, a military/political leader gifted with God's spirit, was supposed to conquer the world and then rule all peoples with justice and compassion. Luke tells us the spirit of God descended on Jesus in the form of a dove after John baptized him. We can think of Jesus' baptism as his inauguration as the messiah because it was then that his heavenly Father gave him the Holy Spirit so he could defeat the devil and begin establishing his reign of justice and peace.

The word "baptism" comes from a Greek word meaning "to immerse in water." In the days of the early Church, Christians baptized by totally immersing the person from head to toe. In imitation of this practice, some modern churches have shallow pools for immersion baptisms, but most modern Christian denominations simply pour water over the person's head.

Water is a powerful symbol of life. It plays a very important role in our own development by first surrounding us in our mother's womb and then refreshing and sustaining us after birth. People in biblical times built towns around a fresh water supply because without water they, their animals, and their crops could not survive. Therefore, water is a very appropriate vehicle through which we receive new spiritual life in baptism.

People living in the dry, hot climate of Palestine were aware of water's cleansing properties. Feet got dirty because most people either walked around barefoot or wore only leather sandals. Water to wash feet was usually the first thing a host offered a guest who arrived after a long journey.

The water of baptism also has cleansing properties, washing us clean of our sins and giving us a fresh spiritual start. Thus, it achieves something ordinary water never could.

Finally, water has a deep spiritual meaning. God used water to save Noah from the sinfulness of the people of his generation and, with water, God prevented the Egyptians from pursuing the Jewish people into the desert. Thus, it is appropriate that God uses the waters of baptism to save us from the power of the devil and to give us everlasting life with him.

For Reflection

The next time you take a bath or a shower, pray for those who do not have running water and have to rely on well water or rainfall for washing, cooking, and drinking. Think of all the uses of running water and thank God for the luxury of modern plumbing.

1st Sunday of Lent

Luke 4:1-13

Modern Christians usually have no trouble acknowledging that Jesus is God, but they find accepting his humanity much more difficult. Hebrews 4:15 tells us we have a high priest (Jesus) who knows what it is to be weak because he, like us, experienced temptation. This means at one time or another Jesus must have had the temptation to lie, to cheat, and to steal. As a man, his head must have turned and his heart must have pounded faster when an attractive woman walked down the street. These are all natural experiences that humans, including Jesus, have encountered since the beginning of time. The only difference is that Jesus never sinned.

Today's Gospel reading tells us about Jesus' struggle with temptation, a story that contains thirteen verses in Luke's Gospel but only two in Mark's. It seems that Luke fills in many of the details while Mark is satisfied with simply saying the devil tempted Jesus. Being much more colorful, Luke's account is the one we are most familiar with.

In the first two of the three temptations, the devil tempts a hungry Jesus to turn stones into bread (a symbol of this world's goods) and he then promises more power and authority if Jesus would only worship him. It would have been easy for Jesus to use his divine powers to fulfill his own desires but he didn't. Instead, throughout the Gospels, we find him using his abilities to serve the poor and the needy.

In the third temptation, the devil takes Jesus to the parapet of the Temple and challenges him to jump. A stairway inside the Temple led to the roof where a seven foot wall (the parapet) ran along the roof's edge. Some biblical scholars think the bricks of the top layer of this wall were pyramid-shaped with sharp spikes sticking out of them to prevent birds of prey (attracted by the smell of the slaughtered animals the priests offered inside to God) from perching there and messing the Temple wall with their droppings.

The story concludes with the devil leaving Jesus until he finds another opportunity to tempt him, indicating Jesus had to struggle with more temptations throughout his life. Temptation, it seems, was just as much a part of Jesus' life as it is part of ours.

For Reflection

All three times when the devil tempted him, Jesus responded by quoting Scripture. What are you doing to become more familiar with Scripture so, like Jesus, you too will be able to fight temptation with God's Word?

2nd Sunday of Lent

Luke 9:28-36

Jesus is at the top of a mountain, deep in prayer, when he changes in appearance. His clothes become dazzling white and Moses and Elijah suddenly appear and converse with him. Half asleep, Peter offers to erect three booths (tents), one for each of the distinguished visitors and Jesus. Without warning, a cloud envelopes them and a voice comes from it. The vision quickly ends and Jesus and the three disciples are alone again.

This Gospel story is rich with symbolism. Some Jews believed the righteous would wear white clothing in God's kingdom and would live in tents because the Jews lived in tents when God led them out of Egypt, through the desert, and into the Promised Land. All this symbolism makes it likely Peter thought he was in the kingdom of God.

The strangest feature of today's Gospel reading is the appearance of Moses and Elijah, two important Old Testament figures who had been dead for hundreds of years. Moses represents the laws God gave him on Mt. Sinai, laws the Jews believed were a guideline to holiness. Some Jews believed following the laws was a sure way to please God and to reserve for oneself a spot in his kingdom. Elijah, on the other hand, was one of the greatest prophets in the history of the Jewish people. Many Jews believed he would return to the earth to prepare the way for the messiah, God's chosen one who would usher in God's kingdom on earth.

Since the Jewish people called their Scriptures (what Christians call the Old Testament) "the Law and the Prophets," we can assume that is what Moses and Elijah represent when they appear together in today's Gospel. We can interpret their presence with Jesus to mean that just as God once worked to save the Jewish people from their physical enemies in the days of the Old Testament, he is now working through his son, Jesus, to save the world from its spiritual enemy, the devil.

All this symbolism points to Jesus being the messiah, a conclusion the voice from the cloud supports when it identifies Jesus as the chosen one (another way of referring to the messiah). The Old Testament sometimes uses a cloud as a symbol of God's presence (see Exodus 13:21, Exodus 16:10, and 1 Kings 8:10-11). Therefore, the voice must belong to the heavenly Father.

Thus, we'll miss the point of today's Gospel if we focus only on the change in Jesus' appearance. What's more important is that the Father used this occasion to confirm Jesus' mission as the messiah, the person he chose to establish his kingdom on earth.

For Reflection

Just as Jesus was at prayer when all this happened, prayer can also transfigure our lives. Identify an area in your life that needs change and ask God to transform you into a new person, pleasing to him in every way.

3rd Sunday of Lent

Luke 13:1-9

In today's Gospel, we hear of two very unfortunate incidents that happened in Jesus' day. First, Roman soldiers killed some Jews who were offering sacrifices in the Temple and then mixed their blood with the blood of the animals the priests offered to God. The second incident involved eighteen people who died when a building collapsed on them. Because the news of these two events was probably on the lips of almost everyone in Palestine, including Jesus and his apostles, some men in today's Gospel ask Jesus for his opinion about what happened.

The Jewish people used their faith in God to explain the meaning of the events in their world, including the tragedies mentioned above. The talk of the town was that God was punishing the victims for sins they (the victims) committed. Their reasoning resulted from a misinterpretation of the Genesis story about the first sin (chapter 3).

Because pain did not become part of life until the man and woman rebelled against God, many people in Jesus' day thought there was a cause-and-effect relationship between sin and suffering, believing sickness and death were God's punishments for sin.

This conclusion sounds logical at first, but Jesus rejects it in today's Gospel.

In the story about Adam and Eve, pain became part of life not as a punishment for sin but as a consequence of it. The difference between punishments and consequences is crucial if we hope to understand this particular story.

Driving his new luxury automobile, an alcoholic speeds down the street at 95 m.p.h., fails to stop at a red light, and runs into a telephone pole as he swerves to miss a pedestrian. The alcoholic suffers a broken leg and totals his new car. A judge suspends his license and orders him to pay a $200 fine.

The broken leg and the wrecked car are consequences of the alcoholic's actions but the fine and suspension are the punishments. This example shows us that consequences naturally flow from an action while punishments are imposed by someone else. We can say that suffering and death naturally flow from living in a sinful world and are not punishments from God for something we did. Therefore, God was not punishing the victims of the two tragedies mentioned in today's Gospel because of a particular sin they committed. Even someone who never sinned would still suffer and die as a consequence of living in a sinful world.

For Reflection

Think of a recent disaster in the headlines. Take time today to pray for the victims and their families.

4th Sunday of Lent

Luke 15:1-3, 11-32

Most Pharisees strictly observed the smallest details of the Jewish laws (a practice they believed made them holier than others) and did not associate with those whom they considered sinners out of fear of being contaminated by these people. In today's Gospel, this group is angry because Jesus does not act the same way. Instead of eating with the Pharisees, Jesus dines with tax collectors and those the Pharisees consider the dregs of society.

First-century Jews who believed God was their king had a strong dislike for tax collectors. The Jews felt outraged when the Roman armies conquered Palestine and declared that the emperor (not the one, true God) would rule over them. As if it wasn't bad enough that this mere human tried to take God's place, he also imposed taxes on the Jewish people, taxes the Jews believed should go to God, their king, for the upkeep of God's house, the Temple in Jerusalem. By collecting taxes, therefore, the emperor was actually stealing from God and the tax collectors were helping him do it. That's why the Pharisees were so angry when Jesus chose to eat with tax collectors instead of respected Pharisees.

In the parable in today's Gospel, the younger son asks for his share of the inheritance. Jewish law entitled the eldest son to twice as much inheritance as his brother(s) because he would become the head of the family and, as such, would have more responsibilities. If there were only two sons, they were supposed to divide the estate into three parts, with the younger son getting one-third of it. Therefore, the younger son in today's Gospel caused a great financial hardship on his family.

After spending his money on loose living, the son gets a job feeding pigs. Since the Jews regarded pigs as unclean animals that they could not eat or sacrifice to God, the son had really hit rock bottom because he was caring for useless creatures.

Returning home, the son asks his father to take him back not as a slave but as a servant. Slaves had more security because they were part of the family and the master had to take care of them. Servants, on the other hand, were not part of the family and could find themselves unemployed and out on the streets at any time.

Rejoicing that his son returned, the father gives him a robe (symbolic of royalty), a ring (a sign of authority and power), and sandals for his feet (worn by important individuals). Thus, he restores the son to his previous position in the family.

For Reflection

Return to your heavenly Father this Lenten season. Give God a chance to welcome you back.

5th Sunday of Lent

John 8:1-11

Since the rabbi was usually the most educated man in a city, the Jews often consulted him whenever they had to make a particularly difficult decision about one of the Jewish laws. In today's Gospel, the scribes and the Pharisees bring such a matter to Rabbi Jesus for his opinion.

According to their law, the Jews were supposed to take anyone guilty of adultery outside the city gates and, depending on the circumstances of the crime, either stone or strangle that person to death. Witnesses to the crime were to be the first ones to carry out the punishment. In today's Gospel, the scribes and the Pharisees come to Jesus with a woman they caught committing adultery and they ask his opinion about what they should do to her.

This situation undoubtedly put Jesus in an uncomfortable position because if he said the woman should die for this offense, some of the Jews would accuse him of not practicing the forgiveness he so often preached about. On the other hand, if he said she should go free, they would charge him with encouraging adultery. It seems like Jesus could not win.

It's not clear what Jesus writes in the sand, but the Greek word the evangelist uses in this passage usually means "to write down a record against someone." Some biblical scholars suggest Jesus was writing a list of the sins of the men who were about to stone the woman. However, this is only a guess and there is no way to know for certain.

After everyone leaves, Jesus tells the woman to go her way but not to commit adultery again. The lesson Jesus wants to teach is clear. We cannot confess our sins and expect God to forgive us unless we intend to avoid those sins in the future. Forgiveness presupposes an effort and a desire to do better.

There are two interesting details missing from today's Gospel story. The evangelist never mentions the man with whom the woman committed adultery but, according to Jewish law, he too should have been condemned to die. Also, the evangelist never names the woman. Nowhere does the Bible ever identify her as Mary Magdalene. Mary has been wrongly accused and never vindicated.

For Reflection

It is easier to condemn than it is to forgive. Identify one person you are critical of. Ask God to help you accept and forgive this person as just Jesus accepted and forgave the woman in this story.

Palm Sunday

Luke 22:14-23, 56

Luke tells us Jesus' sweat became *like* drops of blood as he prayed on the Mount of Olives before his arrest but he does not say Jesus actually sweated blood. Medical experts, however, claim that would have been possible for someone experiencing a great deal of fear. The blood loss, although minimal, would have caused Jesus' skin to become very tender, making the scourging even more painful.

After they arrested Jesus, the chief priest and the Sanhedrin (the Jewish town council in Jerusalem) interrogated him and found him guilty of blasphemy, a crime Jewish law said deserved the death penalty. Although the Roman authorities allowed the Sanhedrin to pass laws, arrest criminals, hold trials, and impose penalties, they reserved for themselves the authority to put someone to death. That explains why the Sanhedrin sent Jesus to Pilate, the Roman governor, and accused him of crimes for which the Romans would execute him.

Pilate ordered the soldiers to scourge Jesus before he decided what to do with him. The soldiers carried out this order with a flagrum, an instrument made of a short wooden handle, leather thongs tied to the handle, and pieces of bone or metal fastened to the other end of the thongs. Because it was possible for someone to die from this punishment, Roman law limited the number of lashes the soldiers could inflict on an individual.

As a military guard led Jesus to the place of crucifixion, he either wore a sign around his neck so everyone would know the crime for which the Roman authorities found him guilty or a soldier carried this sign high in the air for everyone to see. The soldiers later nailed this sign to the cross above Jesus' head.

Because the entire cross would have been too heavy, Jesus carried only the crossbeam (weighing about 125 pounds) on his shoulders as he made his way to the crucifixion site. After the soldiers nailed Jesus to the crossbeam, they lifted it and secured it to a stake sticking out of the ground. This post was shorter than Jesus' body, forcing his torso to hang with knees bent and in a contorted position, not fully stretched out as we usually see in pictures.

Upon arriving at Golgotha, the soldiers probably drove nails through Jesus' wrists, not through his palms because nails through the palms would not have been able to support the body's weight. Death most likely resulted from Jesus no longer being able to expel air from his lungs.

For Reflection

Crucifixion was extremely painful but Jesus endured it out of love for us. Pray that Jesus will help you love him and others more than you already do.

Please refer to Cycle A for the following
commentaries:

2nd Sunday of Easter

John 20:19-31

In the resurrection stories in John's Gospel, the author emphasizes the physical characteristics of Jesus' resurrected body. He does so because some early Christians questioned the idea of a bodily resurrection and said that what the apostles really saw was Jesus' spirit or ghost, not his physical body. Responding to these beliefs, the author of the fourth Gospel was careful to point out that the resurrected Jesus had flesh and bone and that he ate and drank. He wanted to make it clear that the resurrected body was none other than the crucified one.

Today's Gospel begins with all of the apostles except Thomas hiding in a locked room in fear that they would be arrested and killed just as Jesus was. Without warning, Jesus appears in their midst even though the windows and doors are bolted shut. The apostles cannot believe it! They saw him crucified and they saw him die but now he is alive once again!

When Thomas returns, the apostles excitedly tell him all about their experience with the risen Jesus but he refuses to believe them without first putting his fingers in the nail marks in Jesus' hands and in the wound in Jesus' side. Notice that Thomas doesn't say anything about nail marks in Jesus' feet, possibly because the Romans may have used ropes instead of nails to affix a criminal's feet to the cross. Therefore, there wouldn't have been any nail marks in Jesus' feet for Thomas to examine.

Thomas didn't accept what the other apostles told him until he saw Jesus himself. The nail marks and the other wounds were the proof he needed to believe the resurrected Jesus was neither a ghost nor the product of someone's imagination but rather the same Jesus who died on the cross.

Although we will always remember Thomas as the one who doubted, he was actually one of the bravest and most loyal of the apostles. In John 11, there's a story about how Jesus was on his way to Bethany even though he knew there were some men in that city who wanted to kill him. Thomas recognized the potential danger but didn't back away from it; he suggested that he and the other apostles go with Jesus so they could die with him. Whatever Thomas' faults were, cowardice wasn't one of them.

For Reflection

Many times we are like Thomas, wanting to see before we believe. Is there anything about your religion that you have difficulty believing? Take your doubts and questions to Jesus in prayer and ask him to help you believe.

3rd Sunday of Easter

John 21:1-19

One thing that makes the fourth Gospel different from the other three is its rich symbolism. To appreciate what the author wanted to say it is necessary to understand the meaning behind the symbols he chose. Today's reading is a good example of this.

The Gospel story begins with Peter announcing that he is going fishing and Thomas, Nathanael, Zebedee's two sons (James and John), and two other disciples deciding to join him. These men fish all night but catch nothing. Just after daybreak, the resurrected Jesus appears on the shore and calls out to them to lower their nets on the other side of the boat, which they do. Immediately, their nets fill to the breaking point with a total of 153 fish.

Because people in Jesus' day believed there were 153 different types of fish in the world, St. Jerome once suggested that the fish caught in today's Gospel are symbolic of all people and that the net stands for the Church. Just as the apostles found all the different types of fish in their net, we find all the different types of people in the Church, excluding no one.

The story goes on to tell us that six of the disciples haul in the net but Peter alone drags it onto the shore.

The Old Testament often portrays biblical heroes as having superhuman strength (e.g., Samson) because they possess God's spirit. Therefore, the author of the fourth Gospel used this little detail to symbolically show that the Spirit of God was at work in Peter.

When the disciples reach the shore, Jesus offers them some fish and bread, two symbols the early Christians used for the Eucharist. While they are eating, Jesus asks Peter three times if he loves him and three times Peter responds affirmatively. Some biblical scholars suggest that Jesus asked this question three times to symbolically undo the three times Peter denied knowing him.

We find such symbolism in just about every chapter of the Gospel according to John. Taking the time to learn the meaning behind the symbols makes the stories even richer than they already appear.

For Reflection

Jesus gave Peter a second chance. Are you willing to do the same for someone who wronged you? Pray today for the grace to forgive others.

4th Sunday of Easter

John 10:27-30

Since Easter, the Sunday Gospel readings have all had something to do with Jesus' resurrection. Today's reading seems to be an exception until we look at it more closely.

The reading begins with Jesus saying his sheep know his voice and follow him. The Bible mentions sheep over 500 times but that's not so unusual when we consider how important sheep were to everyday life, providing meat to eat, milk to drink, and wool to make clothing. Ancient people even used their horns as containers for oil and as musical instruments.

Because shepherds had a very close relationship with their sheep, all a shepherd had to do was call his sheep and they immediately would come to him even if several flocks had mingled together. These same sheep would not budge an inch if a stranger summoned them.

The sheep in today's reading represent those people who have a very close relationship with Jesus. Jesus promises to give eternal life to his sheep and he says he will never let them perish just as he himself will never die again. In other words, Jesus vows that those who are faithful to him will share in his resurrected life, with death no longer having any permanent power over them either. This eternal life is what we mean when we say we believe in the resurrection of the body and life everlasting.

The reading ends with Jesus claiming he and the Father are one, thus making himself equal to God. The Jews would have considered this assertion blasphemous and their law required them to stone to death the person who spoke these words. Being good Jews, the apostles also would have had problems with this statement unless Jesus had already died and been raised. Only after the resurrection would they have been able to accept what Jesus was saying. Thus, although we find today's reading in the middle of John's Gospel as if Jesus uttered these words before he died, it is more likely John is recalling words the resurrected Jesus spoke to his apostles.

For Reflection

Practice being a good sheep. Learn to recognize Jesus' voice by listening for him. Find a quiet place, get comfortable, and relax. Clear your mind of all distractions and for ten minutes let Jesus speak to you. Don't say anything and don't try to imagine what Jesus would say. Just sit quietly and listen. The more often you do this, the easier it becomes.

5th Sunday of Easter

John 13:31-33, 34-35

Some groups have secret handshakes to distinguish members from non-members and other groups have emblems or distinctive uniforms. The followers of Jesus also have something to set them apart from the crowd, their love for each other. Today's Gospel reading ends with Jesus telling the apostles that their love for one another will be the way other people know they are his disciples. Love is supposed to be what separates them from those who do not believe in Jesus.

A problem arises because the English language uses the one word, love, to describe a wide variety of experiences. We sometimes think of love as a feeling, but we can also use this word to describe many different types of relationships (e.g., the relationship between a parent and child, the relationship between two friends, or the relationship between a husband and wife). This little four letter word can have several different definitions depending on the context within which we use it. With so many possible meanings, how can we know for certain what Jesus had in mind when he spoke the words in today's Gospel?

Although Jesus did not speak English, he may have known three different languages: Hebrew (the official language of the Jewish people), Aramaic (the everyday language of the people of Palestine), and Greek (the language of the Roman empire). Of these three languages, Greek will be the most helpful in determining the type of love Jesus was talking about because it is the language of the New Testament.

There are several different Greek words for our one word "love," including *philia*, a love that describes the relationship between two friends; *eros*, sexual love; and *agape*, a self-giving love. Of these three different words for love, agape is the one we most frequently find on the lips of Jesus. It is also the word for love in today's Gospel.

Agape is a love that focuses on the needs of the other person. It is freely given without counting the cost and without thinking of getting anything in return. Agape looks beyond physical beauty, color of skin, political beliefs, and status. It means reaching out to all people even if they are repulsive or if society considers them worthless. It is the love that should be the hallmark of every Christian.

For Reflection

"See how they love each other!" was the way the non-Christians described the early followers of Jesus. Would non-Christians today say that about your parish community?

6th Sunday of Easter

John 14:23-29

Two people who love each other naturally want to make each other happy. A husband who knows his wife likes freshly cut flowers will occasionally surprise her with a dozen red roses. If he knows she gets furious when he watches football games all weekend, he tries to limit his time sitting in front of the television set so he can spend more time with her. She, for her part, will try not to wake him on a Saturday morning because she knows he likes to sleep in. She'll prepare his favorite meal once in a while, just because.

As if in a married relationship with God, we should base that relationship on love. Just as a husband and wife communicate their likes and dislikes to each other, we communicate our likes and dislikes to God, and God communicates his likes and dislikes to us.

In today's Gospel, Jesus says that if we love him we will be true to his word and that the person who does not love him will not keep his word. In this passage, Jesus tells us how to show our love for him, revealing what pleases and displeases him. The key to this passage, then, is in understanding what it means to be true to Jesus' word.

When we take a good look at what Jesus said and did, we find a single motivation behind every one of his words and actions. Loving all people, even those who are not lovable, is at the heart of Jesus' life and message. Therefore, we should understand being true to Jesus' word to mean we must love others like Jesus loves them. That sounds simple but in reality it's not always easy.

Knowing that loving others may sometimes be difficult, Jesus promises in today's Gospel to send us a Paraclete, the Holy Spirit. A paraclete is someone who stands beside someone else. When we have to do something difficult or scary, it helps to have someone at our side with whom we can share our fears and anxieties, someone who will encourage us and give us support. Jesus sends us his Spirit because peer pressures and fears about what others will think about us may make it difficult for us to be the loving individuals he wants us to be. The Holy Spirit helps us to love when love is not easy.

For Reflection

Think of one person in your life whom you find difficult to love. Pray this week that the Holy Spirit will help you change your attitude about this person. Ask the Holy Spirit to help you love even those who are not lovable.

7th Sunday of Easter

John 17:20-26

When you love someone, you want to be with and share your life with that person. In today's Gospel, Jesus tells us that he loves us so much he wants to share his own divine life with us. He wants to be part of our lives and wants us to be part of his. This is what makes our God different from the other gods of the religions of the world. From the beginning of time, there haven't been many other religions able to claim that their god wanted to establish a close and loving relationship with human beings. Most other religions stressed the strength of their gods. Only Jews, Christians, and Moslems worship a God who is both powerful and loving.

We can compare the close relationship between God and his people to the loving relationship between a husband and wife. Many times, the Old Testament portrays God as a bridegroom and the Jewish people as his beautiful bride. The books of Hosea and the Song of Songs both rely heavily on this imagery.

The New Testament continues this theme, telling us that Jesus spoke of himself as a bridegroom (e.g., Matthew 25:1-13) and sometimes described the kingdom of God as a fantastic wedding celebration open to all who believe in him (e.g., Luke 12:35-40).

Even the way we divide the Bible into two testaments reminds us of God's desire to establish a deeply loving relationship with us. A "testament" is a covenant or agreement in which both parties choose to share their lives with each other in a relationship based on love. Thus, the Old Testament is about the close and loving relationship between God and the Jewish people. (We might be more accurate if we call it the Older Testament because this relationship has not ended but continues to this day.) The New Testament (or Newer Testament) is about the close and loving relationship between God and the followers of Jesus, the Church.

The part of today's Gospel reading that should challenge all Christians is the part in which Jesus prays that his followers will always be united. Apparently, this prayer has not been answered because today the Church is divided into Catholics, Orthodox, Lutherans, Methodists, Presbyterians, and dozens of other denominations. Not only are the divisions according to ideologies but sometimes along racial and ethnic lines as well. Some Christian churches are exclusively for Black people, others are only for White people, and others are for any nationality under the sun. These ideological, racial, and ethnic differences make Sunday the most segregated day of the week. We are a long way from the ideal Jesus prayed for.

For Reflection

Pray this week for Christian unity. Pray that we will one day be able to put aside our ideological, ethnic, and racial differences and worship our God together. Just as love binds Jesus and his heavenly Father, Christians must let love bind them together.

2nd Sunday in Ordinary Time

John 2:1-12

A wedding feast is a biblical symbol for the kingdom of God, therefore, the Old Testament sometimes pictures God as a groom and the people of Israel as his beloved bride. John may have had this imagery in mind when he wrote about the event in today's Gospel.

In this story, there are six stone jars of water the Jews used for ceremonial washings, each with a capacity of about twenty gallons. Some very strict Jews followed a religious law requiring them to wash their hands in a certain way before they ate. With their fingers pointing upwards, they poured water over their hands and let it drip to their wrists. Then, with fingers pointing downward, they poured water so it ran from the wrists to the tip of the fingers. They repeated this ritual before each course of the meal because they believed it was an outward sign of holiness. Hands not cleansed in this way were ritually unclean.

Because wine was both a symbol of joy and an important part of every meal in first-century Palestine, the bride and groom must have been pretty embarrassed when they ran out of it. Jesus may have been at least partially responsible for this shortage if he brought some of his uninvited apostles to the party with him. This would explain why Mary, herself a guest, was so concerned about the shortage of wine.

The six water jars may stand for the special covenant relationship the Jewish people enjoyed with God. Since the number seven was symbolic of perfection, six jars of water meant the covenant was not perfect and had to be transformed by Jesus into an ideal relationship with God in his long-awaited kingdom.

Although the mother of Jesus is a prominent figure in this story, the evangelist never calls her by name in this entire Gospel. At the wedding (and as he hangs on the cross), Jesus simply calls her "Woman," an address that sounds disrespectful to us because there is no precise English translation for the Greek word the Gospel uses here. We may also translate this word as "madam" or "lady" but these titles are much too cold.

Finally, John never uses the word "miracles" in his Gospel but prefers "signs" instead. Today's reading ends when he says the water turned into wine was the first of the signs Jesus performed. John records only seven signs in his Gospel.

For Reflection

We usually see pictures of a serious Jesus but today's Gospel tells us he also went to parties and he undoubtedly had fun at them. We may even assume Jesus and his apostles joked around and teased each other as they traveled from town to town. Today, ask Jesus to teach you how to be a joyful Christian.

3rd Sunday in Ordinary Time

Luke 1:1-4, 4:14-21

In today's Gospel, we find Jesus in a synagogue in Galilee. Since the Gospels mention synagogues and the Temple quite often, we may find it beneficial to distinguish between these two very important Jewish institutions.

There was just one Temple, located in Jerusalem, where the Jewish people could legitimately offer sacrifices to God. At least once a year (and sometimes more often, depending on the distance) pious Jews traveled to Jerusalem to offer the various sacrifices their laws required. These sacrifices were usually cereal offerings (wheat or other grains) or holocausts (animals slaughtered and burnt in whole or in part on the altar of the Temple).

Considering the Temple to be God's home, the Jews ornately decorated it with gold trim, cedar beams, and items of the finest craftsmanship. Since nothing was too good for God, they even stitched the curtain in the Temple with the most expensive thread.

Synagogues, on the other hand, were houses of prayer and instruction. There the rabbis prepared Jewish boys to become adults in their religion by teaching them how to read Sacred Scripture. Jewish men gathered every morning and evening to pray and to hear God's word proclaimed and explained. Unlike the Temple, synagogue was not a place where the Jews could offer sacrifices to God.

According to Jewish law, synagogue services could not begin unless there were at least ten adult Jewish males present. A talk or homily usually followed the prayers and the reading of Sacred Scripture. Because there weren't always officially recognized preachers in the Jewish religion, a prominent citizen or a rabbi trained in Jewish law or Sacred Scripture usually delivered the sermon. According to custom, this person sat as he talked. Questions and a discussion followed.

The process described above is part of today's Gospel. After reading from the book of the prophet Isaiah, Jesus returns to his seat and addresses the congregation. Although the Gospel does not say anything about a discussion and questions, we can assume they followed Jesus' sermon.

Speaking in the synagogue was Jesus' first teaching experience and an opportunity to hone his skills and prepare for his ministry as a wandering preacher. In modern terminology, we can say the synagogues were where Jesus did his student teaching before becoming a certified instructor.

For Reflection

Pray today for priests, deacons, and ministers who are learning to preach. Pray that, like Jesus, they will gain the confidence needed to help others experience God's love.

4th Sunday in Ordinary Time

Luke 4:21-30

During a synagogue service in Nazareth, the town where he grew up, Jesus takes the scroll and reads aloud from the book of the prophet Isaiah. Through the passage he chooses, Jesus claims he possesses the spirit of the Lord and that the spirit is sending him to bring good news to the poor, to set captives free, and to give sight to the blind.

The reference to the spirit of God is the key to understanding what Jesus was talking about. Many Jews believed God would send them a messiah, a military/political leader whom God would anoint with his spirit. This anointed one (that's what "Christ" means) would usher in a new era, a time when the messiah, the champion of the poor, would heal the sick and set captives free. By declaring these things were already happening through him, Jesus was claiming to possess God's spirit and, therefore, was claiming to be the messiah.

Of course, Jesus knew this assertion would not go unchallenged. Those present wanted proof he was indeed who he said he was because other self-proclaimed messiahs at that time disappointed the people who put their faith in them. Thus, we can easily understand why the Jews in the synagogue that day were a little skeptical.

Jesus says that providing proof for his claim would be useless because prophets are usually more readily accepted by strangers than by those who know them the best. One of the greatest Jewish prophets of all time, Elijah, did not go to one of his own people during a famine in the land but helped a poor widow in Zarepath who was not Jewish. Likewise, there were many lepers in Israel, but Elisha (Elijah's successor) helped only Naaman the Syrian. Jesus is saying that no matter what he does, the people of Nazareth will not accept him as the messiah. Therefore, like Elijah and Elisha, he will turn to the Gentiles to manifest God's power in the world and through them he will bring good news to the poor, set captives free, and restore sight to the blind.

For Reflection

The people in Nazareth did not appreciate Jesus because they knew him too well. Identify one person in your life whom you do not appreciate as much as you should. Thank God for giving this person to you.

5th Sunday in Ordinary Time

Luke 5:1-11

Today's Gospel contains one of the best known stories in the New Testament. After preaching to the crowd on shore while drifting in shallow water in Peter's boat, Jesus tells Peter to throw his net overboard. Peter does as Jesus says but he doesn't expect to catch anything. To his surprise, the net fills with so many fish he needs help hauling it in. Peter and his friends then leave their boats and follow Jesus.

Fishing and fishermen have played an important role in the history of Christianity. Some of the twelve apostles were fishermen (Matthew 4:18, Luke 5:6-9, and John 21:3). Although Peter and his partners immediately left everything and followed Jesus, we should not conclude this means they gave up fishing completely. On one occasion, Jesus tells Peter to cast a line into the sea. Peter then finds a coin in the mouth of the fish he catches and uses this coin to pay the Temple tax for himself and Jesus (Matthew 17:27). In another incident, the apostles are in the upper room when Peter announces he is going fishing. A few of the other apostles join him and, while they are in their boats, the resurrected Jesus appears to them (John 21:1-14). These passages suggest the apostles were active fishermen even while they were Jesus' disciples.

A fish also became an early symbol of Christianity because Greek was the most common language in the Roman empire and the letters of the Greek word for fish are i-c-h-t-h-u-s. These are the same letters that begin the Greek words for "Jesus Christ, God's Son, Savior" (*i*esous *ch*ristos *t*heou *hu*ios *s*oter).

The early Christians hung an anchor, another fishing-related symbol, on the door of the houses where they gathered to celebrate the Eucharist. Because it resembled a cross, this secret symbol identified a place where the followers of Jesus could meet to pray and to hear the Word of the Lord.

For Reflection

Peter left his boat behind and followed Jesus because Jesus was even more important to him than his job. What are the three most important things in your life? Does anything come before Jesus?

6th Sunday in Ordinary Time

Luke 16:17, 20-26

Today's Gospel contains part of Luke's account of what we usually call the Sermon on the Mount. However, because it does not take place on the side of a mountain but on a level stretch of land, biblical scholars often call Luke's version of this important teaching the Sermon on the Plain.

The sermon begins with Luke's own narrative of the beatitudes, a variation of those found in Matthew. While Matthew stresses a person's spiritual shape (e.g., the poor in spirit and those who hunger for holiness), Luke is more concerned with one's physical condition (e.g., those who are poor and hungry). Unlike Matthew, who gives us eight beatitudes, Luke mentions only four but adds four woes (e.g., "But woe to you rich...").

Despite these differences, both versions of Jesus' sermon have the same purpose. Many of the Jews in Jesus' day believed the only way to be holy was to follow both the laws in the Torah (the first five books of the Bible) and the 613 laws of the oral traditions (interpretations of the Torah laws). Following all these laws was a heavy burden for poorer Jews who had little time to study them because they had to work many hours a day just to provide for their families. Since an education and knowledge of the laws was a luxury only the rich enjoyed, only the rich could be holy.

The rich believed their comfortable lifestyle was proof God was pleased with them and that God would bless them with places of honor in his kingdom. They believed the poor, on the other hand, experienced many hardships because they were sinners.

In both Luke and Matthew, Jesus shocks his audience by disagreeing with this popular line of thinking. Instead of praising the rich for being holy, Jesus identifies the poor, the hungry, and the persecuted as the ones who will get the places of honor in God's kingdom. This bias towards the lowly is just one reason why Jesus' teachings were so popular with the ordinary people and why the rich and powerful despised them.

For Reflection

We can define "holiness" as "a measure of a person's relationship with God." Therefore, anyone who has such a relationship is holy. How holy are you and what are you doing to grow in holiness?

7th Sunday in Ordinary Time

Luke 6:27-38

The Jewish people believed holiness came from observing all of the laws in Sacred Scripture, so the rabbis created other laws that, if followed, would insure against accidental violation of the biblical laws. The Pharisees treated these man-made laws (known as the oral traditions) as if they were as important as the biblical laws and they thought anyone who did not observe them was a sinner.

Some of the Pharisees accused Jesus of ignoring the Jewish laws because he was often at odds with the oral traditions. In today's Gospel, Jesus defends himself against this charge by pointing out how his teachings go beyond the demands of the law.

The Jewish law commanded love for a neighbor and hate for an enemy and it even permitted a certain amount of retribution. However, in today's Gospel, Jesus teaches his followers to love those who harm them and not to retaliate for an injury in any way, even though the law allows them to do so.

Jesus also instructs his followers that if someone wants to take their coat, they should give that person their shirt as well. People in the first century wore two robe-like garments called a coat (outer garment) and a shirt (inner garment). Palestinian days were warm enough to require wearing only the shirt, but temperatures dropped dramatically after sundown and a person needed a coat to keep from freezing. Because the coat was all a man had to keep himself warm, Jewish law stated that if he used his coat as collateral for a loan, the lender was to return it to him before nightfall. This law protected the poor man from greedy individuals who would do anything to make a profit. Jesus goes beyond the law by telling his audience to give not only their coat but also their shirt, their inner garment, to the unscrupulous lender.

The reading ends with Jesus telling his followers whatever they give to others God will give back to them so abundantly it will overflow the fold of their garment. Because the weight of the robes worn in Jesus' day made it difficult to move about, many people gathered their robe above the belt to allow their legs to move more freely while working. They could then use this material folded over the belt as a kind of pocket for carrying twigs, flour, vegetables, etc. Something so abundant that it overflowed this pocket was plentiful indeed. With this imagery, Jesus wanted to teach us we will receive an abundant reward for all the good we do to others.

For Reflection

In today's Gospel, Jesus tells us we shouldn't return evil with more evil but should do good to our enemies. Do something nice this week for someone with whom you do not get along. How do you think responding with love will affect your relationship with this person?

8th Sunday in Ordinary Time

Luke 6:39-45

In his parables and sayings, Jesus got the attention of his audience by using familiar images. Since farming, herding, and fishing were the three most common occupations in first-century Palestine, the odds were high that there were at least a few farmers, herders, or fishermen in every crowd. Thus, we shouldn't be surprised that Jesus often spoke about such things as sowing seed, herding sheep, and casting a net into the sea.

The parable in today's Gospel is different from Jesus' other parables because he draws upon his own experience as a carpenter instead of tailoring his comments to the interests of his audience. In this story, two men are sawing wood when one of them gets a speck of sawdust in his eye. The other man cannot help his friend because there is a plank blocking his own line of vision. Although Jesus' audience readily understood what he was talking about, the imagery of this parable eludes us because modern machinery has replaced ancient ingenuity.

Since there weren't any sawmills in the first century, men used a rather primitive procedure to turn logs into planks of wood. After placing a log across the tops of two stepladder-like braces, one man climbed on top of the log and the other stood beneath it. Each man then grasped an end of a long saw, pushing and pulling as they cut the log lengthwise. If the man under the log looked up as he was working, sawdust fell into his eye and he was unable to continue. The other man could not get the sawdust out of his friend's eye because his own vision was obscured by the log. This situation is what Jesus was talking about when he said the man could not take the speck out of his brother's eye until he got the plank out of his own.

The speck of sawdust was symbolic of a small fault, while the log or plank represented a more serious problem. Just as the man had to move the log obstructing his own vision before he could help his friend, we must remove from our lives whatever gets in the way of our relationship with God before we can help someone else see God more clearly.

For Reflection

Today's Gospel points to how important it is for our spiritual leaders to lead exemplary lives. Pray today that the priests or ministers who serve your community will be able to remain faithful to the Gospel.

9th Sunday in Ordinary Time

Luke 7:1-10

The Romans divided each legion of their army into sixty groups of 100 soldiers, and they called the man who commanded one of these groups a "centurion." The centurion in today's Gospel is deeply concerned about one of his servants who is deathly ill so he sends some of his Jewish friends to ask Jesus to come heal the man. Normally, Romans and most Jews did not associate with each other because the Jews despised the Romans whose army occupied the land of Palestine and the Romans hated the Jews because they refused to worship Roman gods. However, the centurion in today's Gospel must have been a special person because not only was he friends with the Jewish elders but also he built the synagogue where the Jews gathered for prayer.

As Jesus is on his way to heal the servant, the centurion sends a second message suggesting it isn't necessary for Jesus himself to lay his hands on the man who is sick. The same thing could be accomplished if Jesus simply sends one of his apostles to do the job in his name. The Gospel writer tells us Jesus marveled at this display of faith, but faith may not have been why the centurion made this suggestion.

Very strict Jews in those days did not associate with Gentiles, talk to Gentiles, enter a Gentile's house, or invite Gentiles into their own home because they believed doing so would make them ritually unclean. This meant they would have to go through an elaborate cleansing procedure before participating in religious services. Being aware of this, the centurion sent his second message to avoid putting Jesus in an uncomfortable position. He tactfully advised Jesus to find a way to heal the servant without setting foot in the house himself, thus avoiding criticism from the very strict Jews. The centurion suggested Jesus quietly send one of the apostles to do what he would do in person because everyone would notice if Jesus entered the house of a Gentile, but no one would notice if one of the apostles did the same thing.

For Reflection

The centurion was an important and powerful man, but he was still humble enough to ask Jesus for help. Pray today for the gift of humility so you will be able to rely on Jesus for all your needs.

10th Sunday in Ordinary Time

Luke 7:11-17

Since women in first-century Palestine did not work outside the home, they could never be independent. Although some women did mending and washing for others, what they earned was not enough to support themselves.

An unmarried woman lived in the house of her father who had absolute power over her. If her father passed away, she went to live with her oldest brother or an uncle who usually tried to find her a husband as soon as possible so he would not have to support her. Naturally, if a woman was married, her husband cared for her and protected her. When the husband died, the woman's eldest male child became responsible for her.

Therefore, the woman in today's Gospel had a difficult future ahead of her because both her husband and the only son who had taken care of her were dead. Not only was there no one left to support her, but because she was an older woman with no hope of ever getting married again, it was unlikely that a male relative would take her in and support her for the rest of her life. Under these circumstances, the woman had no choice but to rely on the good will of her friends and relatives until the day she died.

Burial customs in first-century Palestine differed greatly from modern America's customs. After friends or family washed and anointed the body with special aromatic oils, they wrapped it in a linen shroud and carried it to the burial site either on a wooden bier or in a wicker casket made for that purpose. The Jewish people did not embalm their dead because they believed God created the human body in his own image and likeness, making the body holy. Therefore, embalming would have been an act of desecrating that image and likeness. This belief and the hot climate of Palestine made it necessary for burial in New Testament times to take place usually within twenty-four hours after death.

According to Jewish law, anyone who touched the body of the deceased or anything that was in contact with the corpse became ritually unclean and could not take part in the Temple services until they performed the necessary purifications and offered the appropriate sacrifices. Having compassion for the widow, Jesus risks becoming ritually unclean in today's Gospel by going over to the bier and touching it. When the pallbearers stop, Jesus commands the dead man to come back to life. The widow's son immediately sits up and begins to talk.

For Reflection

Sometimes we say people suffer because it is God's will. Today's Gospel tells us God does not like to see people suffer. Our God is a God who has compassion on those who are in need. He does not like to see people in any kind of pain. Pray today for those who suffer in any way.

11th Sunday in Ordinary Time

Luke 7:36-8:3

In first-century Palestine, a host usually welcomed a guest with a kiss of peace. Many people in the Near East and in parts of Europe still follow this custom and greet each other with a kiss on each cheek.

Because Palestine is a dry and dusty land and because people in Jesus' day went barefoot or wore sandals, travelers' feet got dirty. Therefore, a good host either washed the feet of a guest himself or delegated this task to a servant. The host also anointed the guest's head with perfumed oil, a symbol of happiness and pleasure, to show he was happy his visitor had arrived. Apparently, the Pharisee in today's Gospel didn't show Jesus these simple signs of hospitality.

In Palestine, most people opened the doors of their houses in the morning and left them open throughout the day. If a rabbi like Jesus came to visit, it was customary for neighbors to wander in, sit down, and listen to what the rabbi had to say. This explains how the woman in today's Gospel entered the house.

The woman anoints Jesus' feet while he and the Pharisee "recline" at table. As was the custom of the time, Jesus and the other guests were eating while lying on a floor mat on their stomach or side. The food was on a low table, and each guest laid on a personal mat so the head was closest to the table with feet stretched out behind them. This made it fairly easy for the woman to get near Jesus' feet.

The Gospel tells us that Simon, the man who hosted the dinner, was a "Pharisee," a word that means "separated one." The Pharisees got their name because they didn't want anything to do with those who did not follow the Jewish laws as rigidly as they did, fearing contact with these sinners would corrupt them. Evidently, Simon thought Jesus should also separate himself from the woman lest he become like her.

Today's Gospel ends by telling us there were several women who took care of Jesus and the apostles with their own resources. It appears these well-to-do women financed part of Jesus' ministry.

For Reflection

Think of one person you look down upon and don't want to associate with. Like the woman in the Gospel, it's possible this person is closer to God than many other people. Make an effort this week to get to know this person better.

12th Sunday in Ordinary Time

Luke 9:18-24

When Jesus asks his disciples what the crowds are saying about him, they respond that some people think he is John the Baptist. By this time, Herod had already killed John, but Jesus' ministry was so similar to that of John that some people thought he was really the Baptist resurrected.

Others thought Jesus was Elijah (an Old Testament prophet who never died but was taken to heaven in a fiery chariot) or one of the prophets. Some Jews believed Elijah would one day return to the earth to prepare the way for the messiah but there were also some less popular traditions about other prophets coming back from the dead for this same purpose.

Finally, Jesus asks his disciples who *they* think he is, and Peter says he believes Jesus is the messiah. Like many Jewish people, Peter was waiting for a military messiah who would raise an army, conquer the enemies of the Jews, and gain control of the world. God would then use the messiah to establish his kingdom on earth, a kingdom where there wouldn't be any more wars or injustices or suffering. The book of Daniel and today's Gospel call the messiah the "Son of Man."

Jesus did not reject the title of messiah but his understanding of what this person was supposed to be was very different from what many of the Jews expected. In today's Gospel, Jesus paints a picture of a messiah who will suffer and die instead of being gloriously triumphant.

Jesus tells his followers to take up their cross and follow him. To "take up one's cross" was an ancient Jewish expression meaning to trace a cross (a + or X) on one's forehead as a way of dedicating oneself to God. Like a brand that identifies the owner of cattle, this mark showed a person belonged to the Almighty. Those not willing to give themselves completely to God were saving their life for themselves and would lose it but those who gave themselves over to God would save it. Like Jesus, such a person would not be triumphant over human enemies, but would defeat the father of death, the devil himself.

For Reflection

Imagine that Jesus asks you who you think he is. What is your answer? Be honest; don't just give an answer you think Jesus would expect.

13th Sunday in Ordinary Time

Luke 9:51-62

After the death of King Solomon, the Jewish nation divided into two kingdoms with Israel in the north and Judah in the south. In 722 B.C., the Assyrians attacked and captured Israel and sent most (but not all) of the people into exile. Some Jews who remained behind married Assyrian immigrants. Because these people settled in Samaria, we call their descendants Samaritans.

Since the Samaritans were part Jewish and part Assyrian, the Jews despised them and would not allow them to worship in the Temple in Jerusalem. The Samaritans responded by declaring their own temple on Mt. Gerizim the only place where they could legitimately offer sacrifices to God. The Samaritans also used their own version of the Sacred Scriptures during their religious services.

The animosity between Jews and Samaritans was evident in other ways. Because Samaritans were hostile towards Jews who traveled through Samaria, most Jews would not pass through Samaritan territory even if doing so would have saved them several days of travel. Jews who did take a shortcut usually shook the dust from their feet before entering Jewish land so they wouldn't contaminate Jewish soil with Samaritan dirt.

This tension between these two peoples explains why the Samaritans did not welcome Jesus in today's Gospel.

The Gospel ends with a story about three potential followers. Jesus reminds one man that foxes have lairs and birds have nests but he and his apostles have nowhere to live. Being wandering preachers, Jesus and the apostles must have spent many nights sleeping under the stars instead of in a warm, comfortable house. Jesus asks the man if he is willing to give up the security of having a roof over his head in order to be a disciple.

The second man wants to bury his father first, a father who some biblical scholars think was not dead or even close to death. They suggest the man's excuse most likely means something like, "I can't follow you while my father is still alive, but someday he'll be dead and then I'll join you." Jesus rejects this response and challenges the man to put discipleship before everything else, even family.

The third man wants to return home to put his affairs in order. This man is like a farmer who, while plowing his field, risks hitting a large rock or some other obstacle because he keeps looking back. The farmer might hurt himself or damage his plow because he is distracted. We,too, must set our sights on Jesus and not let worldly successes or material possessions divert our attention from our heavenly goal.

For Reflection

The people in today's Gospel let something get in the way of accepting Jesus. What is it that prevents you from being a more committed disciple? Is it security? Family? Success?

14th Sunday in Ordinary Time

Luke 10:1-12, 17-20

Today's Gospel begins with Jesus sending seventy-two men to preach and heal "in his name." Someone who speaks or acts in someone else's name has authority and power from that person so the actions and words of the representative becomes the actions and the words of the person who sent him. That's why Jesus tells his disciples in verse 16 (a verse not in today's reading) that whoever hears them also hears him and whoever rejects them also rejects him.

Exaggeration was a teaching technique rabbis often used in Jesus' day to stress an important point. We find an example of exaggeration in today's Gospel story when Jesus tells the seventy-two they should not greet anyone on the way.

Most Jewish people readily entertained strangers because there are many instances in the Bible in which angels disguised as travelers from distant lands blessed those who showed them hospitality. Therefore, the Jews routinely offered strangers something to eat because there was always the possibility a stranger was really an angel who would bless them for their generosity.

The host often slaughtered, skinned, and then roasted an animal like a sheep or a calf over an open pit or in an earthen oven, delaying the visitor's journey by several hours. When Jesus said the seventy-two should not even greet anyone, he was thinking of the delay that would result if someone wanted to show them hospitality. Therefore, Jesus was telling the disciples their mission to preach the Gospel was so urgent, they were not to postpone it.

The number of men Jesus sends on this mission is also significant. In Genesis 10, we find a list of the nations of the earth. Since there are seventy-two nations on this list, the number seventy-two became symbolic of all the nations of the world. Therefore, Jesus chose seventy-two men to symbolically say his followers had to preach the Gospel to all people.

When Jesus tells the seventy-two he is sending them out like lambs among wolves he is warning them that this task is not going to be easy. This means they are going to experience hostility because of the Gospel and they will even be threatened with physical harm.

For Reflection

The professional religious, like priests and ministers, are not the only ones responsible for preaching the Gospel. Because Jesus also needs you to bring his word to others, your mission is just as urgent as that of the seventy-two. Make up your mind to tell someone about Jesus this week.

15th Sunday in Ordinary Time

Luke 10:25-37

Samaritans were descendants of Jews who married Assyrian immigrants after the Assyrian army captured the northern half of the Jewish nation in 722 B.C. Because the Samaritans were descendants of traitors, the rest of the Jews had nothing to do with them and did not allow them to offer sacrifices in the Temple in Jerusalem. So strong were Jewish feelings toward the Samaritans that Jews who wanted to level the ultimate insult upon someone called that person a Samaritan.

In the parable in today's Gospel reading, a man is on his way from Jerusalem to Jericho, a dangerous journey because thieves often waited along this road to ambush anyone who came by. As can be expected, hoodlums beat and rob the man and then leave him to die. Because this man was coming from the city where the Jewish Temple was located, we can conclude he was probably Jewish.

The first man who comes upon the victim is a priest, a descendant of Aaron (the brother of Moses) whose duty it was to offer sacrifices in the Temple. Because there were so many priests, they drew lots to see who would function in this highly respectable (and sometimes lucrative) role. This priest may have been returning from Jerusalem after completing his term of service in the Temple.

The second man is from the tribe of Levi. Levites were attendants in the Temple and were responsible for cleaning up, filling lamps with oil, assisting the priests, and doing general maintenance work.

The priest and the Levite, both Jews, did not help the man because they were afraid of becoming ritually unclean if the victim was actually dead. According to Jewish law, anyone who touched a corpse was unclean for seven days and could not take part in the Temple services until they performed an elaborate purification ritual and sacrificed an animal to God. The priest and the Levite did not want to risk having to go through all this trouble and expense.

Finally, a despised Samaritan comes along and has compassion on the victim, dressing his wounds and making sure someone takes care of him. This Samaritan was more of a neighbor to the man than the priest and Levite because he went beyond laws and put aside past prejudices when a fellow human being needed him. That's what loving one's neighbor is all about.

For Reflection

At one time or another, most of us have not gotten involved because, like the priest and the Levite, we've said someone else will do it. Pray that you will become more like the Samaritan and always respond with compassion regardless of who needs you.

16th Sunday in Ordinary Time

Luke 10:38-42

Martha and Mary were the sisters of Lazarus, the man Jesus brought back from the dead, and were probably very close friends of Jesus. However, we shouldn't confuse this Mary with Mary of Magdala, another one of Jesus' close friends and the first person to whom he appeared after he rose from the dead. There's nothing in this story or elsewhere in the Bible that links these two women.

Although today's Gospel reading doesn't mention any of the apostles by name, Jesus probably didn't arrive at Martha and Mary's house alone but came with at least some of his apostles. In the Gospel, Martha is angry because she has a house full of hungry men waiting to be fed, and Mary is socializing instead of helping her get the food ready. Martha is stuck doing all the work and she obviously doesn't like it. Most of us would have reacted the same way had we found ourselves in Martha's predicament.

Martha also appears to be a little perturbed with Jesus and it's likely there is at least some anger in her voice when she asks him if he isn't concerned that she is doing all the work while Mary just sits around talking to him. We usually don't like to think of Martha snapping at Jesus like this because, after all, she was talking to God. We forget that Jesus did not walk around with a neon sign on his chest flashing the words, "Worship me, I'm divine!" As far as everyone knew, Jesus was a human being just like they were. He had flesh and bones, he ate and drank, and at times he felt sick. He even had to bathe like everyone else (yes, he may have had body odor after working all day in the carpenter's shop). Since Jesus' followers didn't realize he is also God until after the resurrection, we shouldn't be surprised that Jesus got on Martha's nerves. After all, doesn't that usually happen in a friendship?

Jesus acknowledges that Martha is under pressure because she is trying too hard to prepare a nice meal for her guests. In some ancient manuscripts, the rest of Jesus' words are slightly different from those in today's Gospel. Instead of telling Martha that only one thing is needed (this phrase really doesn't make much sense in the story), Jesus' words may have been "Only a few things are needed (for the meal)," indicating something like, "Don't worry so much about preparing an elaborate feast. Keep it simple. Have a seat and talk to me like Mary is doing because that's what I really want!"

For Reflection

Sometimes the Church needs us to be like Martha, always ready to pitch in and help out. At other times, it needs us to be like Mary, spending time with the Lord. Are you more like Martha or like Mary? Spend time this month cultivating in yourself the qualities of the sister whom you are most unlike.

17th Sunday in Ordinary Time

Luke 11:1-13

Master rabbis (rabbis who trained other men to be rabbis) often taught their students a short prayer they prayed every day as a sign of their solidarity. Like a special theme song or a uniform, this prayer was a sign the person was part of the group. Because John the Baptist taught such a prayer to his disciples, Jesus' apostles wanted a prayer of their own. Jesus responds in today's Gospel by teaching them the Our Father.

In this prayer, we ask God to give us our daily bread. This verse recalls how God fed the Jewish people with manna in the desert after they escaped from Egypt. Each morning, the Jews went outside the camp and gathered only enough manna for that day, showing faith that tomorrow God would once again provide them with their daily bread from heaven. Thus, when we ask God to give us our daily bread we are expressing a trust that he will take care of our everyday needs.

The parable in today's Gospel is about a man who had no food for his unexpected visitors, a most embarrassing situation because Near Eastern hospitality required a host to provide a meal for his guests. So, even though it was the middle of the night, he hurried to his neighbor's house and knocked on the door, hoping to borrow at least a loaf of bread (a food that was part of every meal).

Peasant houses in those days had only one room in which entire families slept together on mats on the floor, surrounded by the family's chickens and livestock. A heavy wooden beam bolted shut the door of the house. Removing this beam would have made much noise and woken the family and all the animals. The havoc that would result might make him pretend not to hear the knocking, hoping the person would go away. Eventually, though, he answered the door because his neighbor refused to give up.

The meaning of the parable should be clear. Just as the man was persistent until his neighbor responded to his needs, we must be persistent when presenting our needs to our heavenly Father. We cannot give up when God does not respond to our prayers as quickly as we had hoped.

For Reflection

Is God interested enough in you to be concerned about your everyday existence or does God only care about the big events or catastrophes in your life? Take time today to tell God about some of the little things that are important to you.

18th Sunday in Ordinary Time

Luke 12:13-21

In today's Gospel, a man asks Jesus to intervene in a legal dispute about how to divide his deceased father's estate. This would not have been unusual because those who disagreed on important matters often called upon rabbis like Jesus to settle their differences.

Jewish Scriptures are made up of two main parts: the Law and the Prophets. The Law, which the Jews called the Torah, corresponds to the first five books of the Christian Bible and contains the rules and regulations God gave to Moses on Mt. Sinai. These laws pertain not only to religious matters but to just about every aspect of daily life as well, including such things as repaying loans, compensating for injuries, and inheriting property. Because of his knowledge of Sacred Scripture, the rabbi was more familiar with the statutes in the Torah than anyone else in the city or town, making him the most logical person to settle a disagreement about how one should interpret or apply a particular law.

A dispute over inheritance was a serious matter in Jesus' day because money and property brought both social and religious status. It's obvious how someone would be able to climb the social ladder if he were rich, but the connection between wealth and one's religious standing needs an explanation.

The Jewish people thought of the laws in the Torah as a blueprint to holiness. Following the laws guaranteed holiness but breaking them, even if one did not know what they were, made a person a sinner. Therefore, holiness was not possible for the ordinary person for two reasons. First, the poor were not educated enough to be able to read the Torah and, secondly, working long hours to support a family prevented the poorer Jews from studying all the laws. A rich man, however, could be holy because he had the time to read the Torah and study the laws. The fact he was rich was proof that God favored him and was pleased with his observance of the law.

Jesus makes it clear in today's Gospel that material wealth does not necessarily translate into spiritual riches. The truly wise person is the one who is more concerned with pleasing God than with obtaining the creature comforts of this world.

For Reflection

Neither money, nor clothing, nor power, nor popularity, nor anything else you value on earth will count when you stand before God's throne. How much time do you spend each day accumulating the good things of this world and how much time do you devote to strengthening your relationship with God? What does this say about your priorities?

19th Sunday in Ordinary Time

Luke 12:32-48

In Jesus' day there were no government insured banks where people could deposit their money for safekeeping, so there was always the possibility thieves would steal a person's entire life savings. Rather than take this risk, many rich people used their wealth to purchase the finest robes money could buy, making expensive clothing an indication of how much a person was worth.

In today's Gospel, Jesus surprises his followers by telling them they are even richer than those who are parading around in costly robes. Their wealth, however, is not like the money thieves steal or like the luxurious clothing moths destroy but is a spiritual treasure their heavenly Father freely gives them. This treasure is nothing less than a place in God's kingdom.

Jesus warns his followers they should always be prepared because they do not know when the kingdom of God (and the final judgment it includes) will come. Therefore, they must always have their belts tightened and their lamps burning.

A person usually fastened a belt around the waist to keep the robe close to the body so it wouldn't flap in the wind. Because the robe extended to the ground and made it difficult to work or move quickly, a person in a hurry tightened the belt and then gathered the robe and tucked it under the belt so it no longer hindered movement. Jesus used this image to teach us that we need to prepare ourselves for the coming of God's kingdom by eliminating anything in our lives that hinders us from moving into a closer relationship with our heavenly Father.

The lamp Jesus spoke about resembled a small ashtray filled with olive oil. A wick floated in the oil and those who depended on the lamp's light had to trim the wick frequently so the flame would not go out, a task that took a great deal of time and effort. In the same way, preparing ourselves for the coming of God's kingdom takes much time and effort because it involves continually striving to love God and love our neighbor more than we already do.

For Reflection

How prepared are you for the coming of God's kingdom? If God should call you to his kingdom today, would he find you with your belt tightened and your lamp burning?

20th Sunday in Ordinary Time

Luke 12:49-53

We usually associate Jesus' message with such things as love and joy and forgiveness, but his teaching in today's Gospel is different. Instead of being hopeful and positive, Jesus warns us of destruction and division. The reading begins with Jesus saying he has come to bring a blazing fire upon the earth and that he will not establish peace, but discord. Jesus even says families will be at odds because of him. This certainly does not sound like the same Jesus who preached about loving one another and turning the other cheek.

Since Scripture often uses fire as a symbol of the judgment at the end of the world, Jesus' comment about bringing fire upon the earth probably meant the day of judgment had already arrived. Jesus challenged those who heard him to make a decision to commit themselves to him and to his message, a decision that would not be without its consequences.

In the days of the early Church, those who professed a belief in Jesus literally put their lives on the line because the Romans killed many Christians by crucifying them, burning them at the stake, feeding them to hungry lions, or skinning them alive. No one would deny that it took a great deal of conviction and courage to be a Christian in first-century Palestine.

Choosing to follow Jesus often had repercussions in one's family life as well. Some parents did not understand why their grown children would risk their lives for the teachings of a simple carpenter from Galilee and some children could not believe their parents had joined a group started by a political radical the Romans crucified. Fathers and sons, mothers and daughters, and mothers-in-law and daughters-in-law found themselves on opposite sides of the fence because of Jesus' teachings. Division, rather than peace, came to many families because of the Gospel.

For Reflection

Christianity often flourishes in countries where it is illegal. Would there be more or fewer Christians in the United States if following Jesus was against the law? Would you be a Christian if you knew you could be physically punished if the wrong people found out about your faith in Jesus?

21st Sunday in Ordinary Time

Luke 13:22-30

In today's Gospel, someone who came to hear Jesus preach asks him if only a few people will be saved. Modern Christians usually interpret this as a question about how many people God will allow into heaven, but it really refers to how many will enter the kingdom of God. Although we often use the terms heaven and kingdom of God interchangeably, they have very different meanings.

Because the Jewish people of Jesus' day understood heaven to be God's home, they believed no one was in heaven except God and his angels. Some Jews believed human beings who led good lives on earth did not go to heaven but had to wait in the land of the dead (also known as Hades or She'ol) until the end of the world when God would reward them by allowing them to enter into his kingdom.

The term "kingdom of God" refers to the time when God will take control of the world and wipe out all pain and suffering. There won't be any more wars or oppression and God will transform the earth back into what it was like before man and woman sinned. God will then invite those who led good lives into this kingdom to enjoy the world as he originally meant it to be but he will leave the wicked outside where they will be wailing and gnashing their teeth. Notice that God's kingdom is not up in the clouds somewhere but is an earthly kingdom separate and distinct from heaven.

The Jews often pictured the kingdom of God as a fantastic banquet in which God will serve the finest foods. Those whom God will invite to this feast will enjoy the honor of sitting down at table with Abraham, Isaac, and Jacob (the three patriarchs of the Jewish people) and will be able to eat all they want without getting sick.

There were many Jews of Jesus' day who thought the kingdom of God as was an exclusive club. Because they were God's chosen people, they believed they were the only ones God would invite to the big feast. God would turn away everyone else at the door. In today's Gospel, Jesus rejects this way of thinking.

Jesus warns his audience that being one of God's chosen people does not, by itself, entitle them a spot in the kingdom. Jesus says it is possible they will be on the outside looking in as many people (even despised and hated Gentiles from the north, south, east, and west) sit at the table enjoying the feast. Therefore, Jesus tells his fellow Jews not to be so smug.

For Reflection

Being a baptized Christian doesn't guarantee we will have a spot in the kingdom of God. We have to be Christian in deed and not just in name. Besides going to church on Sunday, how is your faith in Jesus obvious to those around you?

22nd Sunday in Ordinary Time

Luke 14:1, 7-14

When there is a large dinner banquet, the seating arrangement usually reflects the status of the invited guests. The place of honor is always at the main table with the most important guests sitting next to the host. It was no different in Jesus' day.

In today's Gospel, Jesus warns his audience not to assume they deserve the coveted places of honor because if someone more important arrives late the host may ask them to make room for this person. The resulting embarrassment will be great indeed if the only space left is in the lowliest spot.

The Jews often used a banquet as an image of the kingdom of God. Many of the Pharisees with whom Jesus sat at table believed they deserved the places of honor in God's kingdom not only because they were good Jews but also because of their strict observance of the Jewish laws. Jesus warned them against making this assumption.

In the story Jesus used to illustrate his point, the dignitary who came late and displaced the other man symbolized a sinner. Since many Jews believed sickness resulted from sin, people such as the lame, the blind, and lepers would have been in this category. The displaced guest symbolized the Pharisees who thought they were holier than others.

Jesus' audience would not have missed the point of his message. Jesus was telling the Pharisees they better not be too smug because the people whom they considered sinners might actually be holier and deserving of more honor in God's kingdom. Pride can not only blind us to our own shortcomings but can also make us overlook the good in others.

For Reflection

A woman dreamt that when she died and went to heaven she was surprised to see some people there whom she considered spiritually inferior. She then noticed that each of these people also looked surprised because, it seems, none of them expected to see her there either. Pray this week that God will teach you how to be humble.

23rd Sunday in Ordinary Time

Luke 14:25-33

Like other teachers of his day, Jesus sometimes used exaggeration to emphasize a point. To stress that our loyalty to him is most important, Jesus says in today's Gospel that anyone who wants to be his follower first has to turn his back on parents and family. Jesus does not literally mean we should sever all our ties with those we love but that we shouldn't allow anyone or anything to get in the way of being his disciple.

One of the most misunderstood passages in the New Testament is also part of today's Gospel. Jesus says that whoever wants to be his disciple must take up the cross and follow him, a passage some people interpret to mean Jesus wants us to patiently accept whatever pains and sorrows come our way. Without rejecting this explanation, there is another possible interpretation we should consider.

The Greek word for "cross" in this passage is *tau*, the name of one of the letters in the Greek alphabet. A tau looks something like a + or an X, and the Jews sometimes traced it on the forehead as a way of dedicating themselves to God. Thus, taking up one's tau or tracing the tau on one's forehead meant the person belonged to God just like a brand on a steer indicates it belongs to a particular rancher.

When Jesus says his followers should take up their cross (tau), he means they should give themselves or dedicate themselves to God as the instruments he will use to bring his peace and love into the world. This dedication should be so complete that the person should not allow even family or friends to get in the way of living as Jesus' follower.

Because Jesus realizes what he is asking is not going to be easy, he warns those listening to him that they should first calculate what being his follower will involve. Like the man who built the tower or the king who went into battle, the person who wants to be Jesus' disciple must first determine if it's possible to complete the task, giving up family and possessions, if necessary, for the building of God's kingdom. That's the challenge for us Christians every day of our lives.

For Reflection

Francis of Assisi knew what dedicating one's self to God really meant. Francis' famous prayer begins "Lord, make me an instrument of your peace. Where there is hatred let me bring love; where there is injury, pardon; where there is doubt, faith; where there is despair, hope; and where there is sadness, joy." Do you allow God to work through you, bringing his peace, love, joy, and forgiveness to your family and friends?

24th Sunday in Ordinary Time

Luke 15:1-32

Most city folk might think the shepherd who left ninety-nine sheep in the pasture while he searched for the one that was lost was foolish to leave the flock unattended and vulnerable to attack by wild animals. However, that was not the case. No shepherd would purposely expose his flock to any kind of danger.

Because a very close relationship existed between a shepherd and his sheep, the shepherd gave each of his sheep a name and a sheep came whenever it heard the shepherd calling it. The shepherd in the parable not only knew a sheep was missing but also knew which one it was. This close relationship between the shepherd and the sheep made caring for the animals easier. Several shepherds often combined their flocks in a single pasture and then took turns watching them. They didn't worry about which shepherd owned which sheep. All a shepherd had to do was call his sheep by name and they would come running because they knew his voice. Therefore, the shepherd in today's Gospel did not leave his flock unattended when he went in search of the one that was lost, but left it in the care of another shepherd.

The parable about the woman who swept the entire house looking for a single coin might sound a little ridiculous because it's difficult for us to imagine anyone going through all that trouble for a small sum of money. The explanation for the woman's actions lies in an understanding of ancient courtship and marriage customs.

An unmarried woman often wore a special headband or head covering made of coins or precious jewels that, like a dowry, would go to the man who married her. The headband may have been very elaborate or could have looked as simple as a bent wire on which she strung coins with holes punched through them. The more coins or jewels, the easier it would be for the girl to attract a husband.

A girl like the one in today's Gospel was not rich if she had only ten coins on her headband. Losing one of those coins would greatly reduce her chances of marrying a suitable husband. Therefore, she would sweep the entire house until she found it. She would then have good reason for celebrating.

For Reflection

Both parables end with scenes of great joy. Jesus used these stories to teach that there will be great joy in heaven when we repent and return to our heavenly Father. When was the last time you asked God to forgive your sins?

25th Sunday in Ordinary Time

Luke 16:1-13

In today's Gospel, two men owe a debt to a rich landowner. Although Jesus does not specify the reason for each man's obligation, some biblical scholars suggest the oil and the wheat were probably rent payments. A man who owned land sometimes did not plant crops on it himself but allowed other farmers to work his field in exchange for a percentage of their harvest. If the landowner had vast property holdings or if he did not live near his land, he usually hired a manager to take care of it and collect the rent. A man who did not own the land on which he worked was a tenant farmer.

One of the tenant farmers in today's Gospel grew olives that he later pressed into oil for cooking and for lighting. The other man grew wheat, a very important grain because bread was part of every meal in Jesus' day. Knowing he is about to be fired, the wily manager writes off part of each man's debt, hoping they will remember this when he asks them for help in the future.

The meaning of most of Jesus' parables is clear because each character represents a readily recognizable figure like God, the leaders of the Jewish people, or even the Gentiles. However, it's more difficult to interpret the parable in today's Gospel not only because we cannot easily identify the characters but also because the landowner actually praises the dishonest manager for being clever. Therefore, it's obvious that this parable requires different treatment from other parables because it is so unusual.

Jesus gives us a clue about what he wants to teach when he compares those who immerse themselves in this world to those concerned with other-worldly matters. People put more effort into making money and acquiring possessions than they do in strengthening their relationship with God. They call all the banks in the area to find the best interest or mortgage rate but do little to learn the time and location of a good adult religious education class. They will spend months planning a vacation but cannot find time to attend a weekly prayer meeting or a class on how to meditate. If all of us took our relationship with God as seriously as we take everything else, we would all be saints.

For Reflection

Time management experts claim we will always find time for something important to us. How much time do you spend on religious matters on Sunday in addition to the time you spend at mass? How much time do you spend with God during the week? What does this tell you about how much you value your relationship with God?

26th Sunday in Ordinary Time

Luke 16:19-31

The rich man in today's Gospel must have been extremely wealthy because he dressed in purple and fine linen. Purple dye, which ancient civilizations made from a gland secretion of a certain mollusk, was so rare and expensive that only royalty and the very rich could afford it. Fine linen was also a luxury item.

The Gospel tells us the rich man feasted lavishly every day. People in Jesus' day ate their meals with their fingers because tableware didn't exist. They usually wiped their hands clean with pieces of bread which they then tossed on the ground for the dogs to consume. These pieces of bread are the scraps Lazarus, the beggar, would have been happy to eat.

The rich man died and went to the abode of the dead, a three-layer place under the earth the Jews sometimes called Hades, She'ol, or Gehenna. All who died went to the top layer and waited there for eleven or twelve months until their judgment was complete. If God determined they had led evil and sinful lives, he sent them to one of the two bottom layers (the layer depended on the nature of their crimes) where flames surrounded them and worms ate them. Because the rich man asked for just a drop of water to quench the flames, we can conclude he ended up in one of the two bottom layers.

Those God judged as having lived righteously stayed in the top layer to await their reward. The rabbis argued whether this reward would come at the end of the world or immediately after death. The latter seems to be the case in today's parable because it tells us Lazarus was with Abraham, the father of the Jewish people. Some Jews believed God would honor the righteous by inviting them to a banquet with Abraham in the heavenly kingdom.

The fact that God punished the rich man and rewarded the beggar surprised the people in Jesus' audience because many of them believed wealth was a sign of God's favor and suffering was a punishment for sin. With this parable, Jesus teaches that earthly wealth does not guarantee status in God's kingdom if the rich individual uses the wealth selfishly and ignores the needs of the poor.

For Reflection

How do you use what you have? How much of your wealth do you share with those who are in need?

27th Sunday in Ordinary Time

Luke 17:5-10

Today's Gospel gives us a good example of how Near Eastern teachers like Jesus sometimes used exaggeration to emphasize a point. The apostles ask Jesus to increase their faith and he responds by saying that someone with faith the size of a mustard seed could command a sycamore tree be uprooted and thrown into the sea, and it would happen.

Black mustard bushes grew wild along the shores of the Sea of Galilee not far from Capernaum where Jesus lived during his public ministry and where he did much preaching. Ancient people used the mustard plant for oil, as a condiment, and as an herb, so it was a common ingredient in the foods Jesus and his apostles ate.

Sycamore trees produced a small, yellow, sweet fig-like fruit. Growing along the coast of the Mediterranean Sea made the sycamore the logical choice for the tree cast into the sea in today's Gospel.

In many of the Gospel stories about Jesus' miracles, faith is the reason he is able to make the lame walk, the blind see, and the sick whole. On the other hand, a lack of faith explains the only time in the Gospels when Jesus is not able to heal (Mark 6:1-6).

Recognizing the power of faith, the apostles ask Jesus to give them more of it. Jesus' response is that this is not necessary because even with only a small amount of faith nothing is impossible.

In the second part of today's Gospel, Jesus tells a story about a servant who spends his entire day plowing the field or herding sheep. When the servant returns home in the evening, his work is still not complete because he has to put on his apron, prepare supper, and wait on his master's table. Being a good servant means the master's wishes are more important than his own comfort.

Just as the servant's work is never done, we should never consider our service to God to be complete. There is always more we can do to spread the word about God's love and forgiveness. We can never say we have done our share to build God's kingdom and now it's someone else's turn. We can never take a break from being a follower of Jesus.

For Reflection

Pray today for those who passed on to you their faith in Jesus. Pray for your parents, priests or ministers, religion teachers, and anyone else who helped you develop a closer relationship with the Lord, Jesus.

28th Sunday in Ordinary Time

Luke 17:11-19

In biblical times, leprosy was any skin disease that caused white, crusty patches on the skin. It was not the same as modern leprosy. Since ancient people believed leprosy was contagious, they forced lepers to live outside the city walls and to yell out "Unclean, unclean" whenever a healthy person came near. Any Jew who touched a leper could not take part in religious services until after making certain offerings and performing special rituals. The lepers in today's Gospel did not approach Jesus to ask that he heal them but called out to him from afar.

An interesting detail in today's Gospel is that a combination of Jews and Samaritans, people who normally did not associate or even pray with each other, make up the group of ten lepers Jesus heals. When Jesus tells the lepers to show themselves to the priest, those who are Jewish go to their Temple in Jerusalem and the Samaritans to theirs on Mt. Gerizim. Once in their temples, they would have offered the prescribed sacrifices for someone healed of this dreaded disease and would have performed a rite of purification (Leviticus 14:1-32).

Of the ten whom Jesus healed, the one who returns to thank him isn't a Jew, but a despised Samaritan. He throws himself at Jesus' feet and praises God with a loud voice. To prostrate one's self at someone's feet was symbolic of submitting to that person's authority over you. It was the equivalent of saying something like "Here I am. Do with me as you wish." This gesture was most common when someone entered the presence of a king. Thus, the man was offering himself for Jesus' service. What an appropriate way to thank Jesus for all he had done!

For Reflection

How do you feel when you do something for someone who does not acknowledge or thank you for your efforts? How do you think our heavenly Father feels when we fail to thank him for all he has given us? Make a list of all the things you have and, in prayer, thank God for each of those things individually.

29th Sunday in Ordinary Time

Luke 18:1-8

The Jewish judicial system was different from our own because it did not have judges. In each city or town, the inhabitants chose elders to serve on the town council which not only passed the laws but also tried and punished those who broke them. The Jews called the men who served on this important body elders because they were older men respected by the townspeople for their wisdom and intelligence.

Elders also settled civil disputes between two or more Jews. When neighbors disagreed on property boundaries, people had difficulty paying a debt, or business partners disputed the meaning of the terms of their contract, they brought their disagreements before a panel of three elders who usually listened to both sides of the case while sitting in the town square. Because of human nature and the possibility of bribes, Jewish law did not permit a lone elder to decide a case.

The parable in today's Gospel is about a woman who went to a judge to demand justice. Since there is only one judge in the story and because Jesus does not describe him as an elder, the woman probably brought her case not to the Jewish town council but to a Roman court.

Roman judges were notoriously corrupt and they often ruled in favor of the party who was most powerful and important or who gave the biggest bribe. Therefore, if she was poor and insignificant, there wasn't much chance the widow would win her case. However, when she did not give up but persisted in demanding justice, the judge eventually ruled in her favor so she would stop pestering him.

Just as the features of a champion body builder are more pronounced when he stands next to a 120-pound weakling, the mercy and justice of our God is more apparent when we compare it to the judge in today's Gospel. We can always count on our heavenly Father to treat us as we deserve but we should not give up when he does not respond to our prayers as quickly as we would like. Instead, we have to be as persistent as the poor widow. That's the lesson in this parable.

For Reflection

Sometimes when we ask a friend or family member for something, their response is not always what we expected. Is it possible that God has already answered your prayers but you are not aware of it because he answered in a totally unexpected way?

30th Sunday in Ordinary Time

Luke 18:9-14

The Jews believed God was their king, and they thought their tax money should go for the upkeep of the Temple in Jerusalem (God's house), not to the Roman government for building roads, aqueducts, and pagan temples throughout the empire. Therefore, they treated a fellow Jew who was a tax collector as the most despised sinner because he took what rightfully belonged to God and gave it to the Roman government. To make matters worse, most people suspected tax collectors of collecting more money than they were supposed to and using the excess to bribe their way into better positions.

Thinking the Jewish laws were a way to holiness, the Pharisees followed the oral traditions, a long list of rules and regulations they believed would prevent them from accidentally breaking one of the laws. Treating these man-made laws as if they were just as important as the laws God gave to Moses on Mt. Sinai, the Pharisees labeled anyone who did not observe them a sinner.

This strict observance of the oral traditions separated the Pharisees from everyone else ("Pharisees" means "separated ones"). Some Pharisees even refused to associate with those Jews who did not keep the oral traditions because they feared being corrupted by them. This elitist attitude is why the Pharisee in today's Gospel parable thanks God he is not a sinner like the tax collector.

As proof he is really holy, the Pharisee reminds God that he fasts twice a week and pays tithes on everything he owns. Fasting was symbolic of sorrow for one's sins and tithing (giving a certain percentage of one's belongings back to God) was an act of gratitude for all God's blessings. The Pharisee seems to think fasting and tithing make him better and holier than others.

The parable in today's Gospel shows the stark contrast between the attitude of the Pharisee and that of the tax collector. The Pharisee clearly believes holiness comes from performing the right actions but the tax collector acknowledges his sinfulness and turns to God for forgiveness. Unlike the Pharisee, the tax collector knows holiness is not possible without God. That's why Jesus says the tax collector, not the Pharisee, is justified.

For Reflection

Who do you more closely identify with, the Pharisee or with the tax collector? How much do you depend on God to help you become the person he wants you to be? How much do you depend on your own goodness? Is holiness possible without God?

31st Sunday in Ordinary Time

Luke 19:1-10

Believing God was their king, the Jewish people thought their tax money should pay for the upkeep of God's house, the Temple. Unfortunately, the Roman emperor did not agree with them and used Jewish tax money for building projects throughout the Roman empire. These projects included not only roads and aqueducts in distant lands but also pagan temples to Roman gods; therefore, most pious Jews were greatly upset over how the emperor was using their money.

To make matters worse, the emperor also claimed to be a god. This made paying taxes even more objectionable for most Jews because to do so willingly was just like worshiping a false god, a clear violation of the first commandment.

Oftentimes, Roman officials awarded contracts to foreigners who bid the highest for the privilege of collecting taxes in certain regions. The foreigners then hired local men to do the actual collecting. The Jews called these tax collectors "publicans" and considered any Jew who became a publican the worst kind of sinner because he was helping the emperor steal from God. Other Jews would have nothing to do with such a traitor.

Since a publican had to pay any taxes not collected, he often collected more than he was supposed to, anticipating that some people in his territory would not pay him. The publican either pocketed anything left over after meeting his quota or used the excess to bribe his bosses into giving him a more lucrative territory in which to collect. Thus, Zacchaeus, the chief tax collector in today's Gospel, may have bribed his way to his position and then accepted bribes from the publicans who worked for him.

Zacchaeus' response to Jesus is interesting. According to Jewish law, anyone who steals from someone else and then voluntarily admits it and offers to pay restitution, must pay back what he stole plus twenty percent. The penalty was more if the person did not admit it but was found guilty (Leviticus 6:5; Numbers 5:7). By offering to pay back fourfold and promising to give half of what he owns to the poor, Zacchaeus goes beyond what the law expects of him and shows how sincere he really is.

Not only does Jesus say he will dine with Zacchaeus but he also calls him a son of Abraham, a fancy way of identifying him as a faithful Jew. Jesus was willing to forget about Zacchaeus' past and wipe his slate clean, giving Zacchaeus a chance at a new beginning.

For Reflection

Do you forgive and forget as Jesus did or do you have the memory of an elephant? Ask Jesus to teach you to forgive as he forgave Zacchaeus so you can give someone a chance to start anew.

32nd Sunday in Ordinary Time

Luke 20:27-38

Today's Gospel mentions two religious groups, the Pharisees and the Sadducees. The Pharisees taught that the dead will rise from their graves at the end of the world and at that time God will reward those he judges to have lived good lives by giving them new life in his kingdom. The Sadducees, who were theologically almost the exact opposite of the Pharisees, did not believe in a bodily resurrection or in a life after death. Many of Jesus' teachings had more in common with the Pharisees' beliefs than with those of the Sadducees.

In the long form of today's Gospel, the Sadducees ask Jesus' opinion about a matter that may sound a little strange to us. A woman in first-century Palestine normally could not inherit property, so it was very important for a man to have a son to whom he could leave all his accumulated wealth. If a man died without an heir, his closest male relative was to marry the widow and produce an heir for him. The first male child born of this union would legally be the son of the dead man and would inherit all his property. The Jews called this regulation the Levirate Law (Deuteronomy 25:5-10).

The Sadducees ask Jesus to consider a hypothetical situation. A man who has six brothers dies without having children. The dead man's oldest brother does what the law expects of him and marries the widow but he also dies before a son is born. Likewise, this happens to the rest of the brothers. Since all seven marry this woman, the Sadducees want to know whose wife she will be when everyone rises from the grave at the end of the world. With this question, the Sadducees challenge the belief in life after death.

Jesus first points out that the Levirate Law is supposed to solve a problem in this world (inheriting property) and has nothing to do with what it will be like after the resurrection of the dead at the end of the world. With that out of the way, Jesus then defends his teaching about life after death by quoting a passage from the book of Exodus in which God calls himself the God of Abraham, Isaac, and Jacob. These three men were the patriarchs of the Jewish people and had been dead for almost 1,900 years. Jesus points out that if there is no life after death, then God would have been claiming to be the God of the dead, a claim that would not make any sense because only the living could serve him and give him glory.

For Reflection

The early Christians in the city of Corinth debated about whether or not we will rise from our graves at the end of the world. Look up 1 Corinthians 15:12-19 and read how St. Paul handled this issue. Why is belief in a resurrection so important to Christians?

33rd Sunday in Ordinary Time

Luke 21:5-19

Today's Gospel contains a special type of writing biblical scholars call "apocalyptic," a writing heavy with symbolism intended to give hope to a persecuted people. Because many of the early Christians who heard or read Jesus' words lived in fear of the Romans arresting and/or killing them for their faith, they needed the evangelist to reassure them that Jesus was with them no matter what happened. That, in a nut shell, is the message of today's Gospel.

The reading begins with Jesus and his apostles talking about the Temple in Jerusalem. There was only one Temple and it was God's home, so the Jews used only the best in its construction. They imported the finest wood and marble from distant lands and made the sacred vessels out of the most precious metals. They even made the curtains in the Temple and the high priest's vestments from the most expensive cloth and thread. Nothing was too good for God!

The walls of the Temple were yellow and white marble measuring approximately 177.5' x 120' x 177.5'. Huge plates of gold that reflected the morning sun covered the facade of the Temple, almost blinding anyone who looked directly at the Temple during a sunrise. Gold plates also covered the lower part of each of the other three sides. No other building matched the Temple's magnificent appearance.

Jesus' words about the destruction of the Temple may refer to both a specific historical event and the end of the world. When the Roman army surrounded Jerusalem in 70 A.D., many Christians recalled the words Jesus spoke in today's Gospel and concluded that everything Jesus said was about to come true. Thinking the end of the world was near, they saw no need to defend the city. Instead, they fled to the mountains and let their Jewish neighbors battle the Romans.

Even with the help of the Christians, the Jews would not have been able to prevent the Romans from destroying both the city and the Temple. Nevertheless, this incident caused the already strained relationship between the Jews and the Christians to deteriorate even further until Christianity and Judaism became two completely separate religions.

For Reflection

Jesus was not trying to give us clues about the exact day or hour when the world would end but was reassuring us that we have nothing to worry about if we just put our faith and trust in him. Jesus will be with us whenever and however the end comes.

Trinity Sunday

John 16:12-15

Some modern-day feminists like to refer to God as "she." Although this may sound strange and will probably never become popular, there are biblical passages that do describe God in feminine terms. Isaiah 42:14 and 49:14-15 are just two examples.

Even St. Paul, the New Testament figure feminists call a male chauvinist more than any other, says in Acts 17:28-29 that we live, move, and exist in God because we are his children. Although Paul refers to God with a masculine pronoun in this passage, he seems to be clearly speaking about us being in God's womb because only a child in its mother's womb lives, moves, and exists in someone else.

Notice that today's Gospel refers to the Holy Spirit as "he." Despite this, the Spirit is the most feminine of the persons of the Blessed Trinity. Because this assertion sounds so radical, we definitely need to explain it.

Although the Old Testament does not use the term "Holy Spirit," it does contain many references to the "Spirit of God." Although the Jews did not understand this term to mean the same thing we mean when we speak about the Holy Spirit, it is the foundation for our own teaching about the third person of the Trinity.

Therefore, the way the Old Testament uses this term can shed some light on who the Holy Spirit really is.

The Hebrew words for "Spirit of God" are *ruah Yahweh*. Ruah is a form of the word *ruach*, a Hebrew word that is feminine not only in gender but also in use. Since Hebrew is the language of the Old Testament, this indicates it would be proper to call the Holy Spirit "she."

The Old Testament sometimes also refers to God's Spirit as the Wisdom of God. *Sophia*, the Greek word for wisdom, is another feminine word. By Jesus' day, the Jews translated their Scripture (our Old Testament) into Greek and Jesus often quoted passages from this Greek translation. Therefore, Jesus and the apostles also would have been familiar with this feminine image of the Holy Spirit.

Although the above observations are interesting, they will probably not be enough to convince people to change the pronoun they use for the Holy Spirit. However, these examples should make it easier to respect those people whose mental image of God differs from yours.

For Reflection

Jesus tells us the Spirit will guide us to the truth. Pray that the Spirit will help you to truthfully assess the condition of your relationship with God and to see how that relationship can improve.

Corpus Christi

Luke 9:11-17

Today's Gospel recounts the story of how Jesus satisfies the hunger of a large multitude with just a few fish and a few loaves of bread. Focusing on the great number of people Jesus fed, we often overlook another significant detail. Before giving the food to the people to eat, Jesus raised his eyes to heaven and pronounced a blessing on it (said grace). This blessing was a very important part of every Jewish meal because a pious Jew would not dare eat without first giving thanks to God who gives us all good things.

Although God does not need our thanks, giving him thanks before we eat is a very appropriate response for all he has given us. Recall how you feel when you give something to someone and that person does not acknowledge your gift. The disappointment is bad enough when the ungrateful recipient is a stranger or someone you do not know very well but it is much more acute when the person is someone you love. In such a case, because the gift is an expression of your love, it is easy to feel it is your love, not just the gift, that the person does not appreciate.

With this in mind, we can readily understand how God feels when we fail to give thanks to him for all the gifts he has so tenderly bestowed on us. Because of his great love for us, the pain and the disappointment God feels when we are ungrateful is acute. Our callousness can only communicate to him how little we value his many expressions of love.

Today, on the Feast of Corpus Christi (which is Latin for "Body of Christ"), we celebrate and give thanks to God for the gift of the body and blood of his Son. Since the days of the early Church, Christians have understood the story in today's Gospel to be symbolic of the celebration of the Eucharist. Scripture scholars believe this is the main reason why it is the only story we find in all four of the Gospels.

The greatest gift God could have given us is the gift of his Son, Jesus. Because of his immense love for us, he continues to give us this gift in the form of bread and wine. We take time today to thank God in a special way for this great gift, the gift of his love.

For Reflection

Some people who say grace before meals at home will not do so at a restaurant. Is this right? Would you say grace in a public place? Why or why not?

Christic the King

Luke 23:35-43

Because a king is the embodiment of his kingdom, whatever you do to him, you also do to his subjects. Thus, insulting the king is just like insulting all the people he rules, and honoring him is like honoring the entire kingdom. The king, for his part, acts in the name of all of his subjects. When he forgives or pardons, the entire kingdom forgives or pardons through him.

Being our king, Jesus died on the cross not as an individual but as our representative. In a way, we were also tortured and nailed to the cross with him. That is why Jesus' suffering and death atoned for our sins, something that would not have been possible if Jesus were not our king.

Just as we can say we hung on the cross and died with Jesus, we can also use the same reasoning to claim we have risen from the dead with him. Death no longer has power over Jesus nor any power over us. At the end of the world, we will rise from our graves, never to die again. This is a central teaching of our Christian faith.

In today's Gospel, the crowd, the soldiers, and one of the thieves crucified next to Jesus mock him, contemptuously asking if he is the messiah they are expecting. Because God was supposed to anoint the messiah with his spirit, some of the Jews believed the messiah would lead them in battle against their enemies and would eventually gain control of the world. Jesus, who was neither a successful military leader nor a powerful political figure, failed to meet these expectations when he suffered a very disgraceful death as a common criminal. It seemed like Jesus was the exact opposite of what the messiah was supposed to be.

When the Romans led a man outside the city for crucifixion, a soldier usually went before him carrying a sign announcing the man's crime. The soldier later nailed this sign to the top of the cross. In today's Gospel, the inscription above Jesus' head identifies him as the king of the Jews, a charge that, according to John's Gospel, appeared in Latin, Hebrew, and Greek. In pictures of the crucified Jesus, this sign usually contains the letters INRI, the first letters of the Latin words *Iesus Nazaraenus, Rex Judaeorum*, which means "Jesus of Nazareth, the King of the Jews."

For Reflection

One of the criminals crucified next to Jesus recognized him as the messiah after everyone else gave up on him. How easily do you give up on Jesus when he doesn't respond as you expect? Pray today for the faith to accept Jesus as your own messiah and savior even when things do not go your way.

Holy Days and
Other Feasts

The Presentation

Luke 2:22-40

Today's Gospel talks about two important Jewish religious practices—the purification of a woman after childbirth and the presentation of a male baby in the Temple. Because these two Jewish rituals play an important role in today's Gospel, we must take a closer look at each of them.

The Purification: The ancient Jewish people believed God was the source of life, using blood as a vehicle to communicate that life to human beings. Therefore, a person who came in contact with blood came in contact with God's creative power. Since this experience of God set the person apart from the ordinary world, this individual had to undergo a purification before returning to everyday life. This purification, usually a ritual bath, restored the person to "normalcy" before offering sacrifices to God or taking part in religious services.

Jewish women, therefore, underwent a ritual bath after each monthly period. After childbirth, the woman also offered a year-old lamb and a pair of pigeons or turtledoves at her purification. However, if the woman was poor, she offered only the birds. This explains Mary's offering in today's Gospel.

The Presentation: When the Jews were slaves in Egypt, God appeared to Moses and told him to lead his people to freedom. When the pharaoh refused to let the Jews go, God punished the Egyptian people with ten plagues, the last being the death of the first born Egyptian male in each family. Because God spared the Jews from this catastrophe, they believed their firstborn sons belonged to God (Exodus 13:11-16) and "ransomed" these sons back with an offering of five shekels (coins). In today's Gospel, Joseph and Mary fulfill this Jewish law when they visit the Temple for Mary's purification.

Today's Gospel concludes with Joseph and Mary returning with Jesus to Nazareth in Galilee. Galilee, a region within the land of Palestine where most of Jesus' ministry took place, was a relatively small area, only about forty-five miles long from north to south.

For Reflection

Jesus, Mary, and Joseph's first recorded family outing had a religious purpose. How often does your family pray and attend church services together?

St. Joseph

Matthew 1:16, 18-21, 24 or Luke 2:41-51

Whenever we speak about the parents of Jesus, we almost always focus our attention on Mary and leave Joseph out of the picture unless the discussion centers on the circumstances surrounding Jesus' birth. Because the Gospels say little about Joseph, it's easy to think of him as playing only a minor role in Jesus' life. However, the fact that Jesus preferred to address God as *Abba*, an Aramaic word which means "my father," suggests that Joseph influenced Jesus more than we usually think.

Tell a little child today that God is our heavenly Father, and that child will immediately picture his or her earthly father. If that father is often drunk or abusive, the child might think of God in the same way and will probably grow up fearing God instead of loving him. On the other hand, if the father comes home from work and gives his child a big hug and then later tucks the child into bed, the child will probably picture God as being gentle and caring.

The Gospels make it clear that Jesus thought of his heavenly Father as kind, loving, and concerned about the poor. Jesus probably developed this image of God because he observed these same qualities in Joseph, his earthly father.

By their example, parents teach their children how to love and how to forgive. They also teach them values like honesty, compassion, fairness, and respect for others. Therefore, Joseph could not have taught Jesus how to be loving and patient unless he was a loving and patient parent. He could not have taught Jesus compassion and forgiveness unless he, too, was compassionate and forgiving. Likewise, Joseph could not have taught Jesus the importance of prayer unless prayer was important in his own life.

Although the Gospels do not say much about what Joseph was like, all evidence indicates he was a major influence during Jesus' psychological and religious development. Indeed, he played a much greater role than we usually attribute to him.

For Reflection

Pray for all fathers today. Pray that they, by their example, may lead their children to an understanding of our heavenly Father as a God who is to be loved more than feared.

The Annunciation

Luke 1:26-38

The word "messiah" never appears in today's Gospel, but the author implies it throughout. The Jews expected the messiah to be a descendant of David, whose name shows up in today's Gospel and in today's first reading. David was, at one time, the king of the Jews and a great military leader.

According to 2 Samuel 7, David felt guilty that he lived in a luxurious palace while the Ark of the Covenant (the box containing the tablets of the Ten Commandments) was kept in a tent. Because the Jews believed God was present wherever the ark was, David wanted to build a house (Temple) for both the Ark and the Lord. David abandoned his plans after the Lord revealed to the prophet Nathan in a dream, that he, the Lord, would build a house for David instead. God said this would not be a physical house but a royal household of people. David's kingdom, according to God, would endure forever and his throne would always be firm. The Jewish people believed this meant one of David's descendants would always govern them.

Long after David's death, one enemy after another conquered the Jews, killing their kings and then ruling over them. Since God would not lie and is always faithful, many Jews concluded they had misunderstood the promises he made to David. They reasoned that God would one day fulfill his promises through one of David's descendants. This person would be the messiah.

That is why Luke carefully tells us in today's reading that Mary was engaged to Joseph, who was a descendant of David and that Mary's child will one day occupy David's throne. With these references, Luke shows us that legally (through Joseph) Jesus was a descendant of David and that he was also the messiah. Jesus will rule over the house of Jacob (Jacob was also called Israel; the descendants of his twelve sons make up the twelve tribes of Israel), a rule that will never end.

For Reflection

When Mary agreed to God's request to be the mother of the messiah, God didn't tell her of all the sufferings and disappointments she would experience. Rather, she put her total trust in God's care. Pray this week that you too will find the strength to trust the Lord completely.

The Ascension

Matthew 28:16-20

The early Christians originally passed on the Gospel stories orally and did not write them down until several years after Jesus' death and resurrection. Whenever they gathered to celebrate the Eucharist, they recalled some of the things Jesus said and did, repeating the stories about Jesus for those who were not fortunate enough to have heard him themselves.

First-century Christians sometimes recalled and retold stories that helped them solve a problem. The story about the Pharisees asking Jesus if they should pay taxes to the emperor is a good example. This same question came up in one of the Christian communities and the apostles settled the dispute by recalling Jesus' own response in a similar situation.

Sometimes, the Christians used stories about Jesus to convince others he really was the messiah. In the Acts of the Apostles, we find that they used a short synopsis of Jesus' life to persuade non-believers to repent of their sins, accept Jesus as Lord, and be baptized. Those who did become Christian then studied Jesus' life and teaching in more detail.

Early Christians also repeated certain stories whenever they celebrated the sacraments. For example, they told the story of the wedding at Cana whenever Christians married. They sometimes recalled accounts of miraculous healings when the Christian community anointed and prayed for someone who was sick, especially when that person had the same sickness as someone Jesus healed.

There are two likely reasons why the early Christians preserved the story in today's Gospel. In this reading, Jesus commands the apostles to recruit and baptize disciples from throughout the world. The early Church recalled this story at baptisms but also used it to settle heated debates.

We know from the Acts of the Apostles and from some epistles that the early Christians originally preached only to the Jews. As Paul began preaching the Gospel to the Gentiles, some of the Jews objected to his efforts. When Paul brought this matter to the attention of the apostles, they recalled that Jesus commanded them to go into the world and make disciples from *all* nations. This helped settle the dispute and the early Christians eventually accepted the Gentiles into the Church.

For Reflection

Today's Gospel ends with Jesus' promise to be with us always. Find a quiet spot and for five minutes try to relax and block out all that is on your mind. Focus on Jesus' presence. Make this a daily habit and you'll soon be more aware of Jesus working in your life.

Birth of John the Baptist

Luke 1:5-17 or Luke 1:57-66,80

Although it's unusual for an older woman like John the Baptist's mother, Elizabeth, to conceive and give birth, she was not the only biblical woman to find herself in this situation. There are two other famous mothers who were in similar circumstances.

Sarah, the wife of Abraham, was 86 years old when she gave birth to her son, Isaac. Along with Abraham and Jacob, the Jews revere Isaac as one of the three patriarchs of their people.

Hannah was also advanced in age when she was pregnant with her son, Samuel. When Samuel grew up, he became a great prophet of the Lord who sent him first to anoint Saul and then David as king of the Jewish people.

Just as Isaac and Samuel became God's instruments for changing the course of history, the unusual circumstances surrounding the birth of John indicate God was also setting him aside for an important task. That task was to announce the coming of the messiah.

The Gospels don't tell us anything about John's childhood except that he lived in the desert until he began preaching (Luke 1:80). This detail and the fact he began his preaching near the Jordan River has led some biblical scholars to suggest the Essenes, a group of strict Jews who lived near the spot where the Jordan River flows into the Dead Sea, raised John after his parents died.

The Essenes developed their own community in the desert because they believed an illegitimate priesthood corrupted the Temple worship in Jerusalem. Consequently, they had their own priests who, in accord with Scripture, were descendants of Zadok, the high priest in Solomon's time. Individual Essenes who lived in the community did not own property, but they did practice celibacy and they gathered together regularly for ritual meals. The Essenes believed there would be two messiahs (one political and one religious) and that the world was a battleground for a struggle between the sons of light (good) and the sons of darkness (evil). They also stressed ritual purity through ceremonial washings and strict observance of Jewish laws.

Both John and Jesus probably had contact with the Essenes and were familiar with their teachings. Some of both John's and Jesus' teachings are similar to those of the Essenes, but biblical scholars cannot agree if the Essenes influenced John and Jesus or if the similarities are due to their common Jewish background. The only thing certain is that scholars will be debating this issue for many years to come.

For Reflection

John's task was to point to Jesus, the messiah. Do you say or do anything that points to Jesus being your messiah? Is it obvious to others that you believe in Jesus?

Sts. Peter and Paul

Matthew 16:13-20

In today's Gospel reading, Jesus first asks his disciples what others are saying about him and then he asks them for their own opinion. The various answers to this question tell us there must have been some debate about the meaning of Jesus' ministry.

Some people believed Jesus was John the Baptist. Although King Herod killed John, many people who saw the signs and miracles Jesus performed wondered if he might really be John resurrected. Other people thought Jesus was Jeremiah or Elijah.

Jeremiah was a great Old Testament prophet who took the Ark of the Covenant (the box in the Temple containing the Ten Commandments) and hid it in a cave on Mt. Nebo just before the Babylonians conquered Jerusalem in 586 B.C. (2 Maccabees 2:4-8). Since no one ever found the Ark of the Covenant, some Jews believed Jeremiah would return to the earth just before the messiah's arrival to reveal where he hid it. Thus, Jeremiah's reappearance would indicate that the time of the messiah is near.

Elijah was the greatest of the Old Testament prophets. According to the second book of Kings, Elijah never died but went to heaven in a fiery chariot. Some

Jews believed Elijah would one day return to the world to prepare the way for the messiah. When Elijah appears, the messiah will not be far behind.

The people showed great respect for Jesus when they compared him to these three great men but they did not recognize him as the long awaited messiah. Only Simon Peter understood that Jesus was even more important than the greatest of the Old Testament figures and his belief in Jesus as the messiah earned him a place of honor in the early Church. Simon Peter's faith is the sturdy rock on which the Church is built.

For Reflection

Close your eyes and pretend Jesus is asking you who *you* think he is. What is your answer? Be honest!

The Transfiguration

In today's Gospel, Peter, James, and John witness something very strange when they climb to the top of the mountain with Jesus. Without warning, Jesus' clothing becomes dazzling white, while both Moses and Elijah appear and talk to him. A voice comes from a cloud that overshadows the group. Within seconds, the vision ends.

This vision is rich in symbolism. Moses symbolizes the Jewish laws, while Elijah represents the prophets. Together, they stand for The Law and the Prophets, another name for the Jewish Scriptures. The purpose of the Scriptures is to prepare the world for the messiah who will conquer the world and hand the rule of the world over to God. With God in control, there will be no more pain or suffering or death. The Jews called this the reign or the kingdom of God.

The cloud overshadowing Jesus and his visitors would have reminded the apostles of the column of clouds God used to lead the Jewish people out of Egypt. Thus, the cloud is symbolic of God's presence.

The symbolism in the remainder of the reading also deals with the reign of God. The Jews pictured the saints wearing bright white clothing in God's kingdom, which is exactly how Jesus is dressed.

Peter offers to erect three tents(or booths). Because the Jews lived in tents when they were in the desert on their way to the Promised Land, tents were a symbol of God's saving power. Some Jews believed everyone will live in tents in the kingdom of God.

This symbolism about the reign of God is very important because it points to Jesus being the messiah even though he will not live up to popular expectations. Instead of being the victorious military leader some Jews were waiting for, Jesus was to die the cruel and painful death of a common criminal. By everyone's standards, Jesus was a failure.

In today's Gospel, it is clear the apostles do not grasp the meaning of what Jesus is telling them because as they come down from the mountain we find them discussing what Jesus meant when he said he would rise from the dead. They, too, were looking for a victorious political/military messiah who would not die.

For Reflection

If the apostles had difficulty understanding what Jesus was telling them, it's understandable that today's religious leaders would have difficulty discerning God's will for the Church. Pray that the Holy Spirit will give wisdom to religious leaders so they can discern God's will for his people.

The Assumption

Luke 1:39-56

We sometimes call the prayer Mary says in today's Gospel the Magnificat, a title we get from the first word of the Latin translation of these verses. Although it is a beautiful prayer, the Magnificat is not an original but a combination of several Old Testament passages, similar to the prayer Hannah said when she dedicated her only son, Samuel, to God's service (1 Samuel 2).

God's preference for the poor and the lowly over the rich and the powerful is a theme running throughout the prayer. God confuses the proud and deposes mighty kings, but he looks kindly upon those who are weak and insignificant, raising them to places of honor and giving them their fill of good things.

The Magnificat provides an excellent description of how God has acted throughout history. God constantly chose to work through the least likely candidates. He used Abraham's old and barren wife, Sarah, instead of a young and fertile maidservant to fulfill his promise that Abraham would become the father of a great nation. He sent Moses, a man with a speech impediment, to demand that pharaoh allow the Jews to leave Egypt. He used Rahab the harlot to help the Jews conquer the city of Jericho. Later, God took David, a poor shepherd boy, and made him the greatest king of the Jews.

Mary appropriately rejoices in how God enjoys
working through ordinary people because she too was
poor and lowly. A young girl in her early teens from the
small town of Nazareth in unsophisticated Galilee
would not dare dream that God would have special
plans for her. But God did, and Mary responded
affirmatively to God's power in her life.

For Reflection

Mary did something many women before and after
her did—she gave birth to a child. This birth was
special not only because her child was the Son of God
but because she said yes to God's will in her life. Pray
today that you, too, will have the courage and faith to
say yes to whatever God wants of you. Ask Mary to
pray that you can become more like her, always open to
God's power in your life.

Triumph of the Cross

John 3:13-17

Although the Romans were in control of Palestine in the time of Christ, they permitted the people they conquered to exercise a limited amount of self rule. The Jews in Palestine did this through the Sanhedrin, the town council in Jerusalem, a combination of our Congress and the Supreme Court but for Jewish religious purposes. The Sanhedrin passed laws and then enforced these laws by arresting and putting on trial anyone accused of breaking them. If the Sanhedrin found the accused guilty, it would then prescribe a punishment for the crime. The only restriction the Romans placed on the Sanhedrin was that it could not carry out the death penalty. That was something the Romans reserved for themselves.

In today's Gospel, a man named Nicodemus, a member of the Sanhedrin, comes to visit Jesus at night. This is interesting because the members of the Sanhedrin later arrested Jesus, found him guilty of blasphemy, decreed that he should die for this offense, and then (because they could not carry out a sentence of capital punishment) sent him to the Roman governor with the charge of treason (which, according to Roman law, was punishable by death).

During their late night conversation, Jesus and Nicodemus talk about a bizarre event recorded in the book of Numbers (21:4-9). After escaping from slavery in Egypt, the Jewish people wandered in the desert for forty years. During that time, they experienced many hardships, and some of them even wondered out loud if they made a mistake by leaving Egypt. As a result of their grumbling and apparent lack of trust in him, God allowed a plague of serpents to afflict them. Many who were bitten by one of these serpents died.

When the people repented of their sin, God told Moses to make a bronze serpent and hold it up in the middle of the camp. Those who had been bitten looked at this bronze serpent and did not die.

In today's Gospel we hear that just as Moses lifted up the serpent in the middle of the camp, so must Jesus, the Son of Man, be lifted up on the cross. The meaning of this analogy is clear. Just as those who looked at the bronze serpent regained their health, those who look to Jesus will receive a spiritual healing resulting in eternal life.

For Reflection

A self-proclaimed minister buys tickets to nationally televised sporting events and attends these events wearing a T-shirt that says, "John 3:16." This minister gets seats or positions himself where the camera is sure to focus so people from coast to coast will see his message. John 3:16 is part of today's Gospel reading. Look up the passage. Why does this minister believe this passage is so important?

All Saints Day

Matthew 5:1-12

Since Jews in Jesus' day considered the laws in Scripture and in the oral traditions (the 613 man-made Jewish laws) guidelines to holiness, anyone who wanted to be holy had to follow all these laws. The problem was that the rich had time to study the laws and learn what they meant, but the average person could not do this because he was too busy working long hours just to provide the basic necessities for his family. Therefore, only the rich could be holy. Some Jews considered the way God blessed the rich with wealth and happiness proof he favored them because of their observance of the laws. This favored status supposedly guaranteed them a place of honor in God's kingdom.

In today's Gospel, Jesus surprises a lot of people by saying the rich do not have a monopoly on holiness and therefore aren't necessarily guaranteed the choicest spots in the kingdom. Holiness, according to Jesus, is within the reach of even the poor and the powerless.

Jesus promises the reign of God to the poor in spirit and "the land" (a popular way of referring to the kingdom of God) to the lowly. The persecuted, Jesus says, will receive a great reward and the peacemakers will be known as God's sons, a title the Jews used to describe the righteous who would occupy places of honor in God's kingdom. The people who Jesus said were holy and prominent in the kingdom were the poor and the weak, the same people who were considered sinners because they did not follow all the laws.

Sometimes we fall into the same trap the Jews in Jesus' day fell into and think holiness is just for a certain few like priests, ministers, and those who are "professionally religious." We are afraid to picture ourselves as holy because we don't understand what holiness really is.

Everyone who has a relationship with God is holy and as that relationship becomes stronger, the person becomes holier. Therefore, holiness is like a spiritual yardstick, measuring one's relationship with God. This means that you, me, the person sitting next to us in church, the neighbor who worships at the church down the street, and even the obnoxious kid who is always getting on your nerves may be holy. As Christians, we should all be working on developing a closer relationship with our God and, therefore, should be growing in holiness each day of our lives.

For Reflection

If saints are holy and if you are holy because you have a relationship with God, then you must be a saint. Therefore, rejoice because today the Church celebrates your feast day!

All Souls Day

John 6:37-40; John 11:17-27; or John 14:1-6

Some Jewish people in first-century Palestine believed everyone who died went to a place in the bowels of the earth called She'ol (the Greeks called it Hades). Which of the three layers of She'ol a person eventually ended up in depended on the kind of life that individual had lived on earth.

The top layer of She'ol was the place where the deceased waited until judgment was complete. Judgment lasted eleven months for the righteous but a whole year for the wicked because it took longer for the consequences of their actions to become apparent. The righteous stayed in the top layer to await their reward (the rabbis disagreed about whether the reward would be immediate or if they would have to wait for the resurrection of the dead at the end of the world) but God sent the wicked to one of the two bottom layers where unending flames burned them and worms ate them for all eternity.

Some Jews believed the living could help the deceased by reciting a special prayer, called Kaddish, in the eleven or twelve months before judgment. Although Kaddish was about the coming of the messiah and said nothing about death or the deceased, these Jews believed this prayer had the power to reverse a bad verdict and thus save the deceased from eternal punishment.

The early Christians renamed She'ol "hell" but still pictured it as having three layers. The Apostles' Creed, the oldest creed in Christianity, states that Jesus descended into hell before rising from the dead, meaning he went to the top layer of She'ol to reward the righteous who were waiting there. In time, Catholic Christians began referring to this top layer as purgatory and to only the two bottom layers as hell.

Because many Christians believe heaven is only for those who are perfect, modern Catholic theology explains purgatory as a process in which a person becomes fit for heaven by being purged or cleansed of all imperfections resulting from sin. Just as the Jews recite Kaddish for their deceased, Catholic Christians recite prayers for those who have died in order to speed up the cleansing process. This prepares the deceased for the resurrection of the dead that Jesus speaks of in the Gospel. That is the underlying rationale behind the feast of All Soul's Day.

Because Scripture doesn't clearly spell out the idea of purgatory, Protestant churches do not accept it as an article of their faith.

For Reflection

The communion of saints is the Catholic teaching that we who are living can, through prayer, help those who have died. The deceased, in turn, can pray for us. Spend some time today praying for friends and members of your family who have died in the past year and ask them to pray for you.

Dedication of St. John Lateran

Luke 19:1-10

Just as a king's throne is a symbol of his worldly authority and power, a bishop's chair reminds us of the authority and power the bishop derives from his position within the Church. Because *cathedra* is the Latin word for chair, we call the church in which the bishop's chair is located a cathedral. Each diocese has only one cathedral and it is the mother church of that diocese.

In addition to being the spiritual leader of the Catholic Church, the pope also holds the office of bishop of Rome and, like other bishops, has his own chair. However, because the pope's authority and power extends throughout the world and does not stop at the boundaries of his diocese, his chair and the church in which it is located have a special importance unmatched by other cathedras and cathedrals anywhere in the world.

The pope's chair is in St. John Lateran Cathedral, making this the mother church of Catholic Christianity. Named after St. John the Baptist and located in Rome, Italy, the cathedral was once owned by the Lateran family who gave it to the emperor Constantine (about 324 A.D.). Pope Innocent X rebuilt the church in the seventeenth century and Pope Leo XIII (1878-1903) enlarged it.

Many people mistakenly believe St. Peter's Basilica is the main church of the Catholic faith because it is more well known than St. John Lateran Cathedral. Most public papal liturgies and other religious services officiated by the pope take place in St. Peter's because it is the largest Catholic church in the world and because it is in Vatican City near the pope's residence. Since Rome is usually full of pilgrims who want to be present at these services, the pope uses St. Peter's because it can accommodate more people.

For Reflection

Today's feast is really a celebration in which we acknowledge the pope as the bishop of Rome and the spiritual leader of the Catholic faith, a position that comes with a great deal of responsibility and pressure. Pray today for the Holy Father and for those who advise him on matters affecting the Church and the world. Pray that he will continue to be a strong spiritual leader whose decisions lead others to a closer relationship with God.

The Immaculate Conception

Luke 1:26-38

A few years ago, a television reporter stood in front
of a Catholic church on the feast of the Immaculate
Conception and interviewed people as they entered or
left the church. The reporter asked just one simple
question: "What is the feast of the Immaculate
Conception about?" The responses were embarrassing.

Most of the Catholics interviewed knew it was a
holy day of obligation, but they didn't know why. They
couldn't answer the reporter's question; some didn't
even try. These people were at Mass only because the
Church told them they had to be there.

Other people said the Immaculate Conception
referred to Mary conceiving Jesus in her womb without
sin. Although this was the most frequent response
given, it wasn't the correct answer. Not a single
Catholic there knew what the Immaculate Conception is.

Although today's Gospel reading is about the angel
Gabriel asking Mary to be the mother of Jesus, the
Immaculate Conception has nothing to do with Jesus'
birth. Rather, it's about Mary being conceived in her
mother's womb without the stain of sin. Mary was
sinless from the moment of her conception, and she
remained that way throughout her life, making her the

perfect vessel through which the perfect human being, Jesus, could come into the world.

Parents have the greatest influence in the lives of their children, handing on values, habits, and attitudes to their offspring. Parents teach responsibility and try to instill in their sons and daughters a sense of self worth. They give their children a foundation in the faith and they show them the difference between right and wrong. Children are what they are because of the love and the care parents give them as they are growing up.

Since mothers especially have much influence on their children, we can assume Mary played an important role in the life of Jesus. Along with Joseph, Mary taught Jesus how to love, how to forgive, and how to obey. She taught him compassion and patience and she even taught him how to pray. From the very beginning of her existence, God prepared Mary for this important task, working in her life by molding her and shaping her into the perfect mother and the perfect influence on the savior of the world. That's what we celebrate on the feast of the Immaculate Conception.

For Reflection

Mary knew Jesus better than anyone else knew him. Ask Mary to help you to know and love her son more each day.

Bibliography

Books

Achtemeier, P. J., ed. *Harper's Bible Dictionary*. San Francisco: Harper & Row, 1985.

Barclay, William. *The Daily Study Bible Series*. Philadelphia: Westminster, 1975.

Brown, Raymond E.; Joseph A. Fitzmyer; and Roland E. Murphy, eds. *The Jerome Biblical Commentary*. Englewood Cliffs, New Jersey: Prentice-Hall, 1968.

Catholic Bible Association. Footnotes and introductions to books in the *New American Bible*. New York: Catholic Publishers, 1971.

Hunter, Archibald M. *According to John*. Philadelphia: Westminster, 1968.

Kersten, Rev. John C., S.V.D. Mass themes and biblical commentaries in *New St. Joseph Sunday Missal*. New York: Catholic Book Publishing, 1980.

Packer, James I.; Merrill C. Tenney; and William White, eds. *The Bible Almanac*. Nashville: Thomal Nelson, 1980.

Richardson, Alan. *Saint John*. Great Britain: SCM Press Ltd., 1959.

Articles

Patrich, Joseph. "Reconstructing the Magnificent Temple Herod Built." *Bible Review* (October 1988): 16-29.

Swidler, Leonard. "God, Father and Mother." *The Bible Today* (September 1984): 300-305.

THE MIGHTY MUSTARD BUSH:
Ideas for Biblical Teaching and Preaching
Kenneth Guentert
Paper, $8.95, 140 pages, 5½" x 8½"
ISBN 0-89390-184-9

Whether you need inspiration for a homily or a new outlook on a season, break out your copy of *The Mighty Mustard Bush* and read just one chapter. Need a fresh view on Mystagogia? Try "Drunken Butterflies." Bugged by your congregation's refusal to drink from the common cup? Read "Take My Cup ... Please!" Think the Twelve Steps have a place in liturgy? Read "Jacob's Ladder." The author's biblical sensibility, combined with his down-to-earth wit, will get you going every time.

REDISCOVERING PASSOVER:
A Complete Guide for Christians
Joseph Stallings
Paperbound, $11.95, 352 pages, 5½" x 8½"
ISBN 0-89390-106-7

Relive the history of Passover from its beginnings through modern practice. Along the way, "sit in" on the Passover seder as Jesus celebrated it. In another chapter, the author dispels three popular misconceptions about the Last Supper. This book brings to light the organic connection between the Jewish Passover and the Christian Eucharist.

DISCOVERING MY BIBLICAL DREAM HERITAGE
Lois L. Hendricks
Paperbound, $9.95, 248 pages, 5½" x 8½"
ISBN 0-89390-144-X

In this refreshing approach to Bible study, the author shows you the function of dreams in biblical stories. In non-technical language, she details the dreamers and dreams found in the Hebrew Bible, the Apocrypha, and the New Testament. She then relates them to her own dreams, at the same time guiding you to find the spiritual meaning in yours.

Order these books through your bookseller, or use the order form on the last page.

COPY THIS BOOK!

...and hundreds of other books and songs with an Annual Reprint License.

If you want to reprint pages of this book for any reason—bulletin use, workshops, circulation to parish staff—you can telephone or write for permission each time.

Or you can purchase an Annual Non-Commercial Reprint License from Resource Publications, Inc. (RPI).

The license gives your institution permission to copy hundreds of RPI books and songs, plus articles from *Modern Liturgy* magazine for non-commercial purposes without asking for prior permission. This could save you hundreds of dollars a year in reprint fees, telephone calls, and administrative hassle!

All you have to do is run an appropriate credit line and send a copy at your convenience to RPI's Reprint Department.

That's it. And all it costs is $40 a year. To sign up for the Reprint License, fill out the coupon below or call 408-286-8505 between 8 A.M. and 5 P.M. Pacific Time. License goes into effect after you receive your agreement, license number, and credit-line instructions by return mail.

☐ Yes, I would like your Annual Reprint License. Enclosed is a $40 check or money order.

Name _____

Institution _____

Address _____

City/State/Zip _____

Return to:

Resource Publications, Inc.
160 E. Virginia St. #290
San Jose, CA 95112-5876   BWP

Save Time and Energy
with These Planning Resources

THE MODERN LITURGY PLANNING GUIDE
Robert Zappulla, et al.
Paperbound, $19.95, 438 pages, 6" x 9"
ISBN 0-89390-088-5
A great planning resource for liturgists! You'll receive a Scripture commentary, idea starters, and music suggestions for every Sunday of Cycles A, B, and C of the Roman lectionary—along with seasonal comments and suggestions in a workbook format so that you can retain your notes for the next cycle.

SYMBOLS FOR ALL SEASONS:
Planning Worship Environments for Cycles A, B, and C
Catherine H. Krier
Paperbound, $9.95, 175 pages, 5½" x 8½"
ISBN 0-89390-125-3
Chock-full of environment ideas and descriptions of symbols based on the Sunday lectionary readings of all three cycles, this book also gives you tips on liturgy planning, artistic considerations, and color. Includes space to jot down your own ideas.

THE HOLY WEEK BOOK
edited by Eileen E. Freeman
Paperbound, $19.95, 200 pages, 8½" x 11"
ISBN 0-89390-007-9
Plan more creative Holy Week liturgies with this important resource. It provides historical background, liturgical theology, creative ideas, and more than sixty practical presentations on Palm Sunday, Holy Thursday, Good Friday, and the Easter Vigil. Includes: Palm Sunday parade, several dramatizations of the Passion, instructions for a life-size, build-it-yourself cross for Good Friday, decorations for Easter, children's celebrations, and media suggestions.

WORSHIP THROUGH THE SEASONS: Ideas for Celebration
Mary Isabelle Hock
Paperbound, $8.95, 106 pages, 5½" x 8½"
ISBN 0-89390-104-0
Make your assembly part of the action with help from these songs, dramatic sketches, pageants, movement scripts, and symbolic actions. Includes sections on Advent, Christmas, Epiphany, Lent, Easter, and Pentecost. Easy to follow. Easy to do. Involves children and adults in any congregation.

ADAPTING THE LITURGY:
Creative Ideas for the Church Year
Michael Marchal
Paperbound, $11.95, 295 pages, 5½" x 8½"
ISBN 0-89390-139-3
The author shows you how to adapt the Roman rites— without violating their intent—including both the winter and spring cycles of RCIA as well as many other rites and services throughout the year. Sample adaptations included: Blessing of the Advent Wreath; Christmas Midnight Mass: Lessons and Carols; Renewal of Baptismal Promises on The Baptism of the Lord; Blessing and Distribution of Ashes; Easter Vigil: the Light Service; Renewal of Baptismal Promises on Pentecost; Infant Baptism; Preparatory Rites for First Communion; Healing Service during Eucharist; Blessing for Engaged Couples; Matrimony; and the Rite for Renewing Religious Profession.

IN THE POTTER'S HANDS: Nine Wake Services
Robert Eimer, O.M.I., and Sarah O'Malley, O.S.B.
Paperbound, $6.95 (Bulk prices available), 71 pages, 5½" x 8½"
ISBN 0-89390-132-6
Your wake services must be flexible, interchangeable, and personal if you want bereaved family members to feel spoken to. Choose the most appropriate service by Scripture selection, symbol, theme, or season.

COME, LET US CELEBRATE!
Creative Reconciliation Services
Robert Eimer, O.M.I., and Sarah O'Malley, O.S.B.
Paperbound, $9.95, 87 pages, 7" x 10"
ISBN 0-89390-082-6
These sixteen well-prepared communal reconciliation services are adaptable for Rites II and III of the Roman Catholic sacrament of penance. They have been used in a parish setting and are easy to re-create. Each has symbols and themes carried out in the prayers, homily, examination, scripture readings, and songs. The book also includes twelve ideas that can be used to create additional services.

THE WORD AND EUCHARIST HANDBOOK
Lawrence J. Johnson
Paperbound, $10.95, 140 pages, 6" x 9"
ISBN 0-89390-067-2
A reference guide to the Liturgy of the Word and the Liturgy of the Eucharist. Designed especially for worship planners, ministers, and liturgical artists, it will answer your questions about the origin, development, and modern practice of each part of the Mass.

More Resources for Parish Bulletins, Stationery, and Newsletters!

CLIP ART for Bulletins and Beyond
George Collopy
Paperbound, $14.95
125 perforated pages, 8½" x 11"
ISBN 0-89390-124-5
Produce easy-to-do, eye-pleasing bulletins, banners, and programs with art appropriate for any Sunday of the liturgical year and in various sizes for your convenience. Learn how to use clip art to your best advantage, how to make different bulletins using different folds, and how to enlarge art spots to your specifications. Themes includes the Church, the resurrection, Hebrew Scripture, Jesus Christ, the Trinity, the Cross, and the Virgin Mary.

CLIP ART for Communicating the Good News
Jean Morningstar
Paperbound, $14.95
128 pages perforated, 8½" x 11"
ISBN 0-89390-160-1
These drawings, a remarkable blend of simplicity and inspiration, illustrate passages from throughout the Bible, and cover the seasons of Advent, Christmas, Lent, Easter, Pentecost and many other feasts. The unique format allows you to use them "as is" or in your own designs. Great for stationery, newsletters, student handouts, Sunday bulletins, and flyers.

"The artistic drawings and calligraphy of Sr. Jean Morningstar are a wonderful blend of simplicity and inspiration. I have used her work in school newsletters, invitations, liturgical program booklets, and stationery...in all cases her work is striking and adds greatly to the material." — Br. Frederick Dihlmann, FSC, St. Joseph's Collegiate Institute, Buffalo, NY

ORDER FORM
Order from your local bookstore, or mail this form to:

QTY   TITLE   PRICE   TOTAL

_____

_____

_____

_____

                    Subtotal:_____

CA residents add 7¼% sales tax:_____

(Santa Clara Co. add 8¼% sales tax)

            *Postage and handling:_____

*Postage and handling:
$2.00 for orders up to $20.00   Total amount:_____
10% of orders over $20.00 but less than $150.00
$15.00 for orders of $150.00 or more

Resource Publications, Inc.
160 E. Virginia St., Suite 290
San Jose, CA 95112-5876
or call (408) 286-8505

☐ My check or money order is enclosed.
☐ Charge my ☐ VISA ☐ MC Exp. date:_____

Card#_____-_____-_____-_____

Signature: _____

Name:_____

Institution: _____

Street: _____

City/St/Zip:_____

Code: CC